The Gospels of Mary

The Gospels of Mary

THE SECRET TRADITION OF MARY MAGDALENE,
THE COMPANION OF JESUS

Marvin Meyer

With Esther A. de Boer

HarperOne
An Imprint of HarperCollinsPublishers

HarperOne

THE GOSPELS OF MARY: *The Secret Tradition of Mary Magdalene, the Companion of Jesus.* Copyright © 2004 by Marvin Meyer. All rights reserved. Printed in the United States of America. No part of this book may be used or reproduced in any manner whatsoever without written permission except in the case of brief quotations embodied in critical articles and reviews. For information, address HarperCollins Publishers, 195 Broadway, New York, NY 10007.

HarperCollins books may be purchased for educational, business, or sales promotional use. For information, please e-mail the Special Markets Department at SPsales@harpercollins.com.

HarperCollins Web site: http://www.harpercollins.com

HarperCollins®, 📖 ®, and HarperOne™ are trademarks of HarperCollins Publishers.

FIRST HARPERCOLLINS PAPERBACK EDITION PUBLISHED IN 2006

Library of Congress Cataloging-in-Publication Data is available upon request.
ISBN 978–0–06–083451–7

HB 03.17.2023

Contents

Introduction

OF ALL THE DISCIPLES OF JESUS, none seems to have been as
independent, strong, and close to Jesus as Mary Magdalene.

This book presents English translations of the earliest and
most reliable texts that shed light on this remarkable woman
and the literary traditions about her. These texts include selections from New Testament Gospels, extracanonical literature,
and gnostic sources, including the Gospel of Mary—that is, the
Gospel of Mary Magdalene. Within these texts Mary Magdalene plays a leading role, but often, particularly in the New Testament Gospels, the centrality of her role may be obscured by
the interests of the authors of the Gospels, who advance the
cause of the male disciples (especially the Twelve) and the place
of Peter. When in Matthew 16:18 Jesus is made to say, "You are
Peter, and on this rock I shall build my church," the stage is set
for Peter to assume his primary place as the first of the apostles,
and for the male disciples to take their apostolic places with
Peter as the leaders of the emerging orthodox church. Appropriately, these very words, in Latin translation, occupy a dominant position on the cupola of St. Peter's Basilica in Rome. It is
no wonder that in several of the texts translated here (the

Gospel of Mary, the Gospel of Thomas, Pistis Sophia), Peter himself refuses to accept the teaching and the leadership of Mary Magdalene. While this hostility of Peter toward Mary may not derive directly from their historical relationship, it does reflect conflicting attitudes regarding women's roles and women's leadership in the church. In Peter's world, past and present, it is difficult to accept the important place of a woman, Mary, as teacher and leader.

In his novel *The Da Vinci Code,* Dan Brown has Leigh Teabing and Sophie Neveu discuss these very matters raised by Peter and others in the early Christian texts:

> "The woman they are speaking of," Teabing explained, "is Mary Magdalene. Peter is jealous of her."
>
> "Because Jesus preferred Mary?"
>
> "Not only that. The stakes were far greater than mere affection. At this point in the gospels, Jesus suspects He will soon be captured and crucified. So He gives Mary Magdalene instructions on how to carry on His Church after He is gone. As a result, Peter expresses his discontent over playing second fiddle to a woman. I daresay Peter was something of a sexist."
>
> Sophie was trying to keep up. "This is *Saint* Peter. The rock on which Jesus built His Church."
>
> "The same, except for one catch. According to these unaltered gospels, it was not *Peter* to whom Christ gave directions with which to establish the Christian Church. It was *Mary Magdalene*." (247–48)

In the texts translated in the present book, Mary Magdalene emerges from the shadows of orthodox church tradition as an influential disciple and apostle of Jesus. In the New Testament Gospels, along with the Gospel of Peter, we find a few fascinating stories about Mary Magdalene, and a close reading of these stories discloses features of her life. As best we can reconstruct her background, Mary Magdalene was a Jewish woman from the city of Magdala on the western shore of the Sea of Galilee, and her nickname ("Magdalene") refers to her hometown. Magdala was well known for fishing and fish salting. Thus, the Aramaic name of the city is Migdal Nunya (or the like), "Tower of Fish," and the city was given the Greek name Tarichêa (in Latin, Taricheae), "Salted Fish." Some have sought to derive Mary's nickname "Magdalene" directly from the Aramaic word for "tower," *migdal,* and to suggest that Mary "Magdalene" is Mary "the Tower," but this is a difficult interpretation.[1] She is simply Mary Magdalene, Mary of Magdala, from the city Magdala, or, in her Aramaic name, Miryam of Magdala.

Mary Magdalene is on the scene in the New Testament in Luke 8, where she is an independent woman traveling with Jesus, along with two other women, as part of the Jewish Jesus movement. There is no mention of husbands or family members accompanying these women. They are on their own, with Jesus and friends. All three women are said by Luke to have been restored to health through Jesus, and of Mary it is said that Jesus cast seven demons from her. This statement employs the language of magic, miracle, and exorcism, and it reflects the interests of the author of the Gospel. If the account reflects any historical reality, it may imply that Mary faced social, mental, or spiritual issues, and that Jesus helped her address those needs. So, it is intimated, Mary Magdalene becomes a disciple of Jesus, and her status in the circle of those around Jesus is alluded to by the fact that she is nearly always listed first among the women following Jesus. The single exception to this pattern in the New Testament is John 19:25, where the concern seems to be that women of Jesus' family be listed first. Further, according to Luke, Mary Magdalene and her women friends provide support and assistance for the Jesus movement from their personal resources. Some interpreters have suggested that Mary's life-style and economic means may indicate that she is widowed or divorced; or perhaps she is a self-sufficient and self-reliant woman living on her own. As Carolyn Osiek puts it in *Women in Scripture,* "This was a strong woman" (122).

According to the Gospels of Mark, Matthew, Luke, John, and Peter, Mary Magdalene remains loyal to Jesus even during the final difficult days, and she is present at the crucifixion and the tomb of Jesus. In some Gospel accounts, the male disciples run for their lives when Jesus is crucified but Mary and other women linger in the vicinity of the site of the execution. On Sunday morning, the accounts maintain, Mary Magdalene goes to the tomb of Jesus, sometimes with one or more other women, to embalm the body and mourn for Jesus. And in the longer ending of Mark (16:9–11), and in John 20:1–18, Mary Magdalene becomes the first person to encounter the risen Christ and proclaim the good news of the resurrection. In the Gospel of John, the account of this meeting of Mary Magdalene and Jesus is tender and loving, with a gently erotic tone. Jesus says, "Mary," and Mary responds, "Rabbouni." Mary departs to announce the resurrection to the other disciples, and from this act she has become known in the tradition as the apostle to the apostles.

In the other texts published in this book, the significance of the role of Mary Magdalene as a disciple of Jesus, and a beloved disciple, becomes even more apparent. In the New Testament Gospels the inner group of disciples often takes on the charac-ter of a male-only club, with restricted membership. Other texts, however, show that this was not the case. According to these texts, there were both male and female disciples around Jesus, and the Gospel of Mary, the Gospel of Thomas, the

Gospel of Philip, the Dialogue of the Savior, and Pistis Sophia all depict Jesus associating equally with men and women. In the Gospel of Thomas 61, Salome observes that Jesus has climbed onto her couch (or bed) and has eaten from her table, and she says to Jesus, "I am your disciple." Jesus in turn speaks words of wisdom and knowledge to her. In all these other texts Mary Magdalene, too, is treated as a disciple and can be addressed as a disciple of Jesus, and at times she is acclaimed to be the disciple Jesus loves most. In the Gospel of Philip not only is it said that Jesus loves Mary Magdalene more than the other disciples; Mary is also called the companion, partner, or consort of Jesus, and the text states that Jesus kissed Mary frequently.

In the light of such statements, it seems entirely appropriate to call Mary Magdalene a beloved disciple. That title is most familiar from the Gospel of John, where the beloved disciple is an important if vague figure in the Johannine story line. A great deal of ink has been spilled in scholarly efforts to understand and identify the beloved disciple in the Gospel of John. He—or she—may be a fictional character (so Hans-Martin Schenke) or an ideal figure (so Rudolf Bultmann) or a symbol of the believer (so Raymond E. Brown). The situation is complicated in the Gospel of John, however, and the beloved disciple also seems to take on the responsibility of eyewitness and even Gospel author; and without a doubt the beloved disciple is related, literally, to Lazarus, and through Lazarus to the youth in the Gospel of Mark and Secret Mark who is also said to be a beloved disciple.[2]

Furthermore, other Christian texts also depict beloved disciples, and these texts often identify the beloved disciple with one person or another. In the Secret Book (or Apocryphon) of James and the First and Second Apocalypses of James from the Nag Hammadi library, James the Just, the brother of Jesus, is portrayed as a beloved disciple, and in the Gospel of Thomas and the Book of Thomas, also from the Nag Hammadi library, Judas Thomas is the twin of Jesus and a beloved disciple. Similarly, in the Gospel of Mary, the Gospel of Philip, and elsewhere, Mary Magdalene is understood and identified as a beloved disciple.

And possibly even *the* beloved disciple, if Esther A. de Boer is correct. In her essay "Mary Magdalene and the Disciple Jesus Loved," de Boer argues that Mary Magdalene is very possibly the beloved disciple in the Gospel of John. She begins by noting previous arguments that identify Mary Magdalene as the beloved disciple and the author of the Gospel of John, and she goes on to offer subtle points of interpretation. In John 19:25–27, for instance, Jesus sees his mother and the beloved disciple, and he talks to them from the cross. He addresses his mother as "woman" (in Greek, *gynai*) and says to her, "Woman, look, your son," but he never addresses the beloved disciple as "son." This leads de Boer to the conviction that when Jesus tells his mother to look at her son, he actually means that Mary should look at her son Jesus. De Boer continues, "The ultimate importance of the scene in 19:26–27 lies in Jesus' invitation to his mother to look away from her dying son to find him, alive, in the disciple he loved." The veil of anonymity that obscures the beloved disciple in John, de Boer maintains, stems from repressive elements in John, elements that question the authority of female discipleship, and as a result it is hard to perceive the figure of Mary Magdalene in the beloved disciple. De Boer writes:

I conclude that Mary Magdalene should be seen as a serious candidate for the identification of the anonymous disciple Jesus loved in the Gospel of John. If we indeed look upon her as an important candidate, this has consequences for our general perspective on Mary Magdalene. She would have had disciples, her testimony would have formed a community, her accounts not only of the death and resurrection of Jesus, but also of his life and teachings, would have been preserved. But not only that, her words would have been canonized and taught through the ages, and spread over the world.

If Mary Magdalene is a beloved disciple, possibly even *the* beloved disciple, how was she beloved to Jesus? If the portrayal of intimacy between Mary and Jesus applies to their historical relationship, were they physically intimate with each other? There certainly are erotic hints throughout the literary sources—in John 20, in the Gospel of Mary, and particularly in the Gospel of Philip. And while a reasonable case can be made that Jesus may have been sexually active and perhaps even married, and that Mary Magdalene, the woman who was closest to him, is the single best choice of a woman who may have been his lover, the evidence remains inconclusive. The intimate tone of John 20 ends with a request of Jesus: "Do not touch me." The love between Mary and Jesus in the Gospel of Mary seems more platonic and spiritual. The kissing and loving of the companions or partners in the Gospel of Philip is described within the context of the spiritual and sacramental interests of the text. In all these passages, of course, a spiritual understanding of love could have been imposed upon the texts by authors and editors who preferred a less physical sort of love and intimacy with Jesus. So, Mary and Jesus may indeed have experienced physical love with each other, or they may not. We cannot know. After all, as the Gospel of Philip reminds us, "No [one can] know when [a husband] and wife have sex except those two, for marriage in the world is a mystery for those married."

Nikos Kazantzakis struggles with these questions in *The Last Temptation of Christ* when he narrates his version of the relationship between Mary Magdalene and Jesus. In Kazantzakis's novel, Mary is a whore who has known Jesus from childhood and who becomes a follower. In one of the last scenes in the novel Jesus swoons on the cross and fantasizes about his last temptation, the everyday life of sex and family, the ordinary life of the flesh with Mary Magdalene:

> Purring, Mary Magdalene hugged the man, kept his body glued to hers.
>
> "No man has ever kissed me. I have never felt a man's beard over my lips and cheeks, nor a man's knees between my knees. This is the day of my birth! . . . Are you crying, my child?"
>
> "Beloved wife, I never knew the world was so beautiful or the flesh so holy. It too is a daughter of God, a graceful sister of the soul. I never knew that the joys of the body were not sinful."
>
> "Why did you set out to conquer heaven, and sigh, and seek the miraculous water of eternal life? I am that water. You have stooped, drunk, found peace. . . . Are you still sighing, my child? What are you thinking about?"
>
> "My heart is a withered rose of Jericho which revives and opens up again when placed in water. Woman is a fountain of immortal water. Now I understand." (450)

In Kazantzakis's novel, in the account of this scene of dream and hallucination, Mary Magdalene dies, and Jesus goes to Mary the sister of Lazarus. "In the humid half darkness the faces of Mary Magdalene and Mary sister of Lazarus were mixing, becoming one" (457). Jesus lives with and loves Mary and Martha, and they have children. Yet this narration of the last temptation of Jesus, and the last temptation of Kazantzakis, memorable as it is in the novel and the film based on the novel, stays in the realm of imagination. Jesus imagines the relationship with Mary Magdalene, and Mary and Martha, and in the end he does not give in to the temptation. He rejects the everyday life of marriage and children and accepts the cross.

Ultimately, in the texts considered in this book, the question of sex is not the most significant thing about Mary and Jesus. In these traditions, it is neither sex nor gender that defines Mary. But for Peter, in the stories about his animosity toward Mary, Mary is specifically defined by her gender. For Peter, Mary is a woman who does not know her place. And for those interpreters who identify Mary Magdalene with the unnamed woman of Luke 7:36–50, said to be a woman of sin, who washes Jesus' feet with her tears, dries them with her hair, and kisses and anoints his feet with perfume, Mary Magdalene is also defined by sex and gender. In this interpretation she is a whore who comes to Jesus and to repentance, but she *is* a whore, and much of the literature regarding Mary Magdalene, like Kazantzakis's *Last Temptation of Christ,* reflects this interpretation.

The portrait of Mary in literature and art as reformed whore is impressive, but it is mistaken in terms of historical accuracy and literary interpretation. It may also have the effect of marginalizing Mary Magdalene by reducing her role to that of a repentant prostitute, and such an effort at marginalizing Mary may have been deliberate. It was not until the late sixth century that Pope Gregory the Great formally identified Mary Magdalene with the prostitute of Luke 7, and the identification stuck. There is, in fact, no good reason to identify Mary Magdalene with the unnamed prostitute of Luke 7, just as there is no good reason to identify Mary Magdalene with the unnamed woman of Bethany in Mark 14 or Mary of Bethany, sister of Lazarus, in

Luke 10 and John 11–12. The faces mix and blend in Kazantza-kis's fantasy, and in Pope Gregory's identification, and such mixing of Mary Magdalene with other women is just as much a matter of fantasy in other interpreters.

If the image of Mary Magdalene in many of the texts gath-ered here transcends the issues of sex and gender, the implica-tions for the ongoing discussion of sex and gender in society and religion are clear. In the world of Mary Magdalene, past and present, sex and gender do not define a person or limit a person's participation in society and religion.

What is most significant about Mary Magdalene in the early literary sources is that she is a close follower and beloved disci-ple of Jesus, and she assumes the role of an articulate advocate for the gospel, and an eloquent leader of the faith, regardless of her gender. In the Gospel of Mary, when the other disciples are weeping and are discouraged at the departure of Jesus, it is Mary who is strong. She lifts their spirits by assuring them that the grace of Jesus will remain with them and protect them. She encourages them to praise the greatness of Jesus, and to remember that they have been made adequate for what is to come. They are true human beings, Mary proclaims. In other words, the Gospel of Mary says, "she turned their hearts to the good." It is Mary who recounts and understands the revelatory vision of the soul and its fate, and she communicates this vision to the rest of the disciples. In contrast to the belligerence of Peter and his brother Andrew, it is Mary who is the model of the spiritual teacher.

Appropriately, in the Dialogue of the Savior, Mary, described as a leading disciple in conversation with Jesus and the other disciples, utters wisdom sayings attributed elsewhere to Jesus, and she is described as "a woman who understood everything [or "completely" (in Coptic, *eptêr'f*)]." In Pistis

Sophia, Mary, presented as the most prominent of all the disciples, provides insightful interpretations of sayings of Jesus and passages of scripture, and she proclaims the nature and meaning of salvation. Jesus tells Mary, "You are one whose heart is set on heaven's kingdom more than all your brothers," and he says again, "You are more blessed than all women on earth." Mary is, Jesus insists, "pure spiritual woman [or "pure spiritual one" (fem.); in Coptic, *tepneumatikê 'nhilikrines*]." And in the Manichaean Psalms of Heracleides, Mary is praised as the one who cast the net to gather the lost disciples, and she is, the poet declares, "the spirit of wisdom."

Karen L. King provides an excellent summary of the character of Mary Magdalene as teacher and leader in her essay "Why All the Controversy? Mary in the *Gospel of Mary*":

> The portrait of Mary Magdalene in the *Gospel of Mary* offers an alternative to sole reliance on apostolic witness as the source of authority. Although she, too, knew the historical Jesus, was a witness to the resurrection, and received instruction from the Savior, these experiences are not what set her apart from the others. Mary is clearly portrayed throughout the *Gospel* as an exemplary disciple. She does not falter when the Savior departs. She steps into his place after his departure, comforting, strengthening, and instructing the others. Her spiritual comprehension and spiritual maturity are demonstrated in her calm behavior and especially in her visionary experience. These at once provide evidence of her spiritual maturity and form the basis for her legitimate exercise of authority in instructing the other disciples. She does not teach in her own name but passes on the words of the Savior, calming the disciples, and turning their hearts

toward the Good. Her character proves the truth of her teaching, and by extension authorizes the teaching of the *Gospel of Mary*—and it does so by opposing her to those apostles who reject women's authority and preach another gospel, laying down laws beyond that which the Savior taught. (73–74)

In addition to the early Christian texts presented in this book, there are more texts and traditions that expand upon the story of Mary Magdalene and develop it in intriguing and sometimes spectacular directions. In the Acts of Philip, a certain woman named Mary (Mariamne), called the "sister" of the apostle Philip, is a leading figure in the second half of the text, and she is involved in healing—her saliva is the healing agent—and teaching and administering sacraments. Philip baptizes men; Mary baptizes women. Mary is arrested for her beliefs and practices, but before she can be stripped and humiliated, her body is transformed into a box of glass. François Bovon, who has studied the Acts of Philip extensively, is convinced that this Mary or Mariamne is Mary Magdalene. If that is true, the stories in the Acts of Philip may indicate a continuation of traditions concerning the role of Mary Magdalene as teacher and leader in the early church. According to Epiphanius of Salamis, a heresiologist who often seems both naïve and mean-spirited, there was another text, entitled Great Questions of Mary, in which Jesus has a revelatory encounter with Mary, apparently Mary Magdalene, and performs an act based on the story of Eve separating from Adam in Genesis 2. Epiphanius claims that in the text Jesus separates a woman from his side, has sex with her, and takes his semen as the seed of life to be used ritually. Mary, it is said, is shocked and collapses, but Jesus raises her and says, "Why did you doubt, you of little faith?" While these statements from the Great Questions of Mary may reflect the close relationship between Mary and Jesus and the reception of teachings from Jesus, the brief account seems to develop these ideas in the direction of the sort of libertine story that Epiphanius loves to tell about the wicked gnostics he says he is exposing.

There are numerous other later tales and legends about Mary Magdalene, curious and intriguing legends that are incorporated in *The Da Vinci Code,* in *Holy Blood, Holy Grail,* and in *The Woman with the Alabaster Jar.* In these texts it can be said that Jesus and Mary Magdalene were married, that they had children, that the holy grail *(san graal)* is actually the royal bloodline *(sang raal)* of Jesus, and that the descendants of Jesus have had a powerful impact upon history. Perhaps Mary herself is the holy grail. Perhaps Jesus did not really die on the cross, a suggestion also made in gnostic and Islamic sources. Perhaps his wife, Mary, and their children moved to Marseilles or elsewhere in France, eventually to influence the royal houses of Europe. And perhaps Mary Magdalene has a coded name that, by gematria, identifies her as a fertility goddess or a sacred woman or a manifestation of female sexuality. Perhaps she was a priestess of Ishtar or Inanna or Isis. Perhaps she is linked to Venus and the *hieros gamos* or sacred marriage.

Perhaps. Or perhaps not.

The sources about Mary Magdalene published here may not be as flamboyant as some of these later legends, but they are more trustworthy as witnesses to the figure of Mary and literary traditions about Mary. And they are provocative enough. In these sources Mary Magdalene confronts us anew, and her presence and proclamation are compelling. It is said that she knew Jesus intimately and spoke on his behalf, and she continues to speak in words recorded in the Gospel of Mary: "Do not weep or grieve or be in doubt, for his grace will be with you all and will protect you. Rather, let us praise his greatness, for he has prepared us and made us truly human."

※ ※

This book is entitled *The Gospels of Mary* because it presents early sources that proclaim the good news, or the gospel, according to Mary Magdalene, in the literary traditions that reflect upon her. The literary sources on Mary Magdalene presented here include the Gospel of Mary and selections from the Gospels of Mark, Matthew, Luke, John, Peter, Thomas, and Philip, from the Dialogue of the Savior, and from Pistis Sophia, as well as a song from the Manichaean Psalms of Heracleides. Three other texts, two of which are from the Nag Hammadi library, also make mention of Mary, but the references are brief, general, and somewhat uncertain. In the Epistle of the Apostles (Epistula Apostolorum, 11), Mary tells the disciples about the resurrection of Christ in a way that recalls Mary Magdalene in other Gospel accounts, including the Gospel of Mary. In the fragmentary First Apocalypse of James it is claimed that Jesus had twelve male disciples and seven female disciples, and Mary is mentioned by name (Mariam, 40). In the Wisdom of Jesus Christ (or the Sophia of Jesus Christ), Mary (Mariamme) is said to have asked two questions of Jesus, one regarding how the disciples can come to knowledge (98), the other regarding the nature of the life of discipleship (114). These three texts add little more than this on Mary, and they are not included in the translations that follow, though the three texts are discussed in the essay by Esther de Boer.

The texts presented here are all translated into English by the author. The selections from the Gospel of Thomas, the Gospel of Philip, and the Dialogue of the Savior incorporate somewhat more material from those texts in order to provide a fuller context for the presentation of Mary Magdalene. The selections from the New Testament Gospels do not provide as much additional material beyond the references to Mary Magdalene, since these biblical texts are readily available and may be easily consulted. Relevant numbers of chapters, verses, sayings, and Coptic manuscript pages, enclosed in parentheses, are included for the sake of ease of reference. Within the translations, square brackets indicate textual restorations and pointed brackets indicate textual emendations. Notes are added to explain difficult passages and to refer to parallel passages.

✸ ✸

I would like to express my gratitude to Chapman University and the Griset Chair in Bible and Christian Studies for the continued generous support of my research, including the research on this book. Several of the translations in this book have been undertaken as a part of a larger research project on the Nag Hammadi library, and for that project John Loudon and HarperSanFrancisco have been particularly helpful. Several collaborators in that project, including Wolf-Peter Funk, Birger A. Pearson, Paul-Hubert Poirier, James M. Robinson, and John D. Turner, have offered insightful comments on some of the translations published here. Finally, I thank Esther de Boer for her valuable essay included in this book. As she concludes, the texts published here reveal that Mary Magdalene "was a crucial disciple of Jesus with her own distinct role and Gospel," and the study of these texts, canonical and non-canonical, "allows Mary finally to emerge from the shadows of history."

CHAPTER I

The Gospels of Mark, Matthew, Luke, John, and Peter

THE GOSPELS OF MARK, Matthew, Luke, and John are the four New Testament Gospels, and the Gospel of Peter is a related fragmentary Gospel. All five Gospels were apparently composed during the last decades of the first century C.E. Among the New Testament Gospels, it is generally assumed that the Gospel of Mark was written first, around 70 C.E., and that the Gospels of Matthew and Luke were written a decade or two later and made use of a version of the Gospel of Mark as one of their major literary sources, along with the sayings source Q, a source similar to the Gospel of Thomas. The Gospel of John was written around 90 C.E., and it differs rather substantially from the Gospels of Mark, Matthew, and Luke. Nonetheless, there are points of connection between Mark and John in particular, and all four New Testament Gospels narrate a story of Jesus that emphasizes the crucifixion and its aftermath. So does the Gospel of Peter, which also announces the good news—the gospel—of the cross.

Mary Magdalene figures rather significantly in the New Testament Gospels and the Gospel of Peter. In Luke 8 (and the longer ending of the Gospel of Mark) she is said to be one of the women whom Jesus restored to social, mental, or spiritual health, and it is reported that he cast seven demons from her. There she is in the company of other women who are followers of Jesus, and Luke depicts Mary Magdalene and friends as independent women who travel with Jesus and provide support for the Jesus movement. Mark 15:40–41, written prior to Luke, uses different language and may allude to the women as disciples.

In all the New Testament Gospels it is said that Mary Magdalene is present at the cross and at the tomb of Jesus. In Luke there is only the general statement, in the context of the crucifixion account, that the acquaintances of Jesus and the women from Galilee were standing at a distance. Mary Magdalene's prominence is highlighted by the fact that ordinarily she is mentioned first in lists of women around Jesus. John 19:25 is an exception to this pattern, and two or three women are referred to ahead of Mary, but these women seem to be relatives of Jesus. According to Mark 15 and Matthew 27, Mary Magdalene and another woman named Mary saw the burial place of Jesus (again Luke gives a more general statement). It is maintained in all five gospels—Mark, Matthew, Luke, John, and Peter— that Mary Magdalene, often in the company of other women (though not in John), comes early on Sunday morning to the tomb of Jesus. In Mark 16 Mary and the women see a youth in the tomb; in Matthew 28 they are frightened by an apocalyptic angel; in Luke 24 they are greeted by two men in dazzling clothes.

The very first of all the followers of Jesus to experience the risen Christ, according to Mark 16 (the longer ending) and John 20, is Mary Magdalene. According to Matthew 28, Mary Magdalene and "the other Mary" share the experience. In John 20 the account of the encounter between Mary and Jesus is emotional and the exchange of words is tender. Jesus' command that Mary not touch him has sparked a goodly amount of discussion, with several possible interpretations. This command may show the concern of Jesus (and the author of the Gospel) with the unclean nature of Jesus' body, since he died so recently, or with Jesus' need to return to the father, or with matters having to do with sexuality.

The scene in the Gospel of John seems to express such intimacy that it may recall the description of a woman seeking her lover in Song of Songs 3:1–5:

> Night after night on my bed
> I dreamed of my lover.
> I was looking for him
> but could not find him.
> "So I shall rise and wander through the city,
> down streets and through markets.
> I shall look for my lover."
> I looked but could not find him.
> The watchmen came upon me
> as they patrolled the city.
> I asked, Have you seen my lover?
> No sooner had I left them
> than I found my lover.
> I held him, I would not let him go,
> till I brought him to my mother's house,
> to the chamber of her who conceived me.
>
> Promise me, daughters of Jerusalem,
> by the gazelles and swift deer of the field,
> that you will not arouse, will not awaken my love,
> until love is ready.[1]

The selections from Mark, Matthew, Luke, John, and Peter translated here feature texts that specifically and unequivocally concern Mary Magdalene. Other texts that portray the unnamed woman who is said to be a woman of sin and who washes Jesus' feet with her tears, dries them with her hair, kisses them, and anoints them with perfume (Luke 7:36–50), an unnamed woman who anoints Jesus at Bethany (Mark 14:1–9), and Mary of Bethany (Luke 10:38–42; John 11:1–5, 17–20, 28–35; 12:1–8) are also included as additional stories about women around Jesus. These stories may be related to each other in some way, but they are not about Mary Magdalene. Some interpreters, however, have attempted to link these unnamed women and Mary of Bethany to Mary Magdalene, and for that reason these texts are also presented here, though they are placed separately after the selections on Mary Magdalene. The selections from the Gospels of Mark, Matthew, Luke, John, and Peter are given one after another in a series of translations. They should not be harmonized into a single account; their differences reflect the differing perspectives of the several authors.

FOR FURTHER READING: Raymond E. Brown, *The Gospel of John;* John Dominic Crossan, *The Cross that Spoke;* John Dominic Crossan, *Four Other Gospels;* Esther A. de Boer, *The Gospel of Mary;* Helmut Koester, *Ancient Christian Gospels;* Burton Mack, *A Myth of Innocence;* Maria Grazia Mara, *Évangile de Pierre;* Carol Meyers, Toni Craven, and Ross S. Kraemer, eds., *Women in Scripture;* Robert J. Miller, ed., *The Complete Gospels;* Susanne Ruschmann, *Maria von Magdala im Johannesevangelium;* Jane Schaberg, *The Resurrection of Mary Magdalene.*

The Gospels of Mark, Matthew,
Luke, John, and Peter[2]

MARY MAGDALENE AND OTHER WOMEN
PROVIDE SUPPORT FOR JESUS

Luke 8:1–3

(1) It happened soon afterward[3] that Jesus was traveling through the towns and villages, preaching and announcing the good news of God's kingdom. The Twelve were with him, (2) as well as some women who had been cured of evil spirits and diseases: Mary, called Magdalene, from whom seven demons had departed,[4] (3) and Joanna, the wife of Chuza, Herod's steward,[5] and Susanna,[6] and many others, who supported[7] them[8] with their resources.

MARY AND OTHERS ARE PRESENT
AT THE CRUCIFIXION OF JESUS

Mark 15:33–36

(33) When it was noon,[9] darkness covered the whole land until 3 o'clock in the afternoon. (34) At 3 o'clock Jesus shouted with a loud voice, "Eloi, Eloi, lema sabachthani," which means, "My God, My God, why have you abandoned me?"[10]

(35) Some of the bystanders heard it and were saying, "Look, he is calling Elijah." (36) And someone ran and filled a sponge with cheap wine, put it on the end of a stick, and offered it to Jesus to drink, and said, "Wait, let us see if Elijah comes to rescue him."

John 19:25—27

(25) Standing by Jesus' cross were his mother, his mother's sister, Mary the wife of Clopas,[11] and Mary Magdalene. (26) Jesus saw his mother and the disciple he loved[12] standing there, and he says to his mother, "Woman, look, your son."[13]

(27) Then he says to the disciple, "Look, your mother." From that moment the disciple took her into his home.

Mark 15:37—41

(37) Jesus gave a loud cry and breathed his last.

(38) The temple curtain was torn in two from top to bottom. (39) When the Roman officer stationed at the cross saw how Jesus died, he said, "This person really was God's son."

(40) There were some women looking on from a distance, among whom were Mary Magdalene, and Mary the mother of James the younger and Joses, and Salome.[14] (41) They used to follow Jesus and assist him while he was in Galilee. Many other women who came to Jerusalem with him were also there.

Matthew 27:55—56

(55) Many women were there, looking on from a distance. They had followed Jesus from Galilee to assist him. (56) Among them were Mary Magdalene, Mary the mother of James and Joseph,[15] and the mother of the sons of Zebedee.[16]

MARY AND OTHER WOMEN AT THE TOMB

Mark 15:42—47

(42) When night had fallen, since it was preparation day, the day before the Sabbath,[17] (43) Joseph of Arimathea, a respected council member who himself was awaiting God's kingdom,

came forward.[18] He went boldly to Pilate and requested the body of Jesus. (44) Pilate was surprised to hear that Jesus had died so soon, and he summoned the Roman officer and asked him if Jesus had been dead for long. (45) When he heard the officer's report, he let Joseph take the body. (46) Joseph bought a linen shroud and took the body of Jesus down. He wrapped it in the shroud and put it in a tomb hewn out of rock, and he rolled a stone in front of the entrance to the tomb. (47) Mary Magdalene and Mary the mother of Joses saw where Jesus was laid to rest.

Matthew 27:61

(61) Mary Magdalene and the other Mary[19] were sitting there, facing the tomb.[20]

Peter 12:1–5

(1) It was early on Sunday morning, and Mary Magdalene, a disciple[21] of the master, was afraid of the Jews, since their anger was aroused,[22] and so she did not perform at the tomb of the master the rites that women usually perform for their departed loved ones. (2) Instead, she took her women friends with her and went to the tomb where the master had been placed. (3) They were afraid the Jews would see them, and they were saying, "Although on the day the master was crucified we could not mourn and beat our breasts, now let us perform these rites at his tomb. (4) But who will roll away for us the stone placed at the entrance to the tomb, that we may enter and sit by him and do what ought to be done?" (5) For the stone was large. "We are afraid someone will see us. And if we cannot move the stone ourselves, at least let us set at the entrance to the tomb the memorial we brought for the master, and mourn and beat our breasts until we return home."

Matthew 28:1

(1) After the Sabbath, toward dawn on Sunday, Mary Magdalene and the other Mary[23] went to see the tomb.[24]

Mark 16:1–8

(1) When the Sabbath was over, Mary Magdalene, Mary the mother of James, and Salome bought spices so they could go and embalm the body of Jesus. (2) Very early on Sunday morning, at sunrise, they went to the tomb. (3) They were asking themselves, "Who will roll away the stone for us from the entrance to the tomb?" (4) Then they look up and see that the stone has been rolled back—it was very large.

(5) When they entered the tomb, they saw a youth,[25] sitting on the right and wearing a white robe, and they were alarmed.

(6) The youth says to them, "Do not be alarmed. You are seeking Jesus of Nazareth, who was crucified. He has been raised, he is not here. Look at the place where they put him. (7) But go and tell his disciples, including Peter, he is going ahead of you to Galilee. There you will see him, as he told you."

(8) And the women went out and fled from the tomb, for terror and fright overcame them. They did not say a word to anyone, for they were afraid.[26]

Matthew 28:8–10

(8) The women hurried from the tomb, with fear and great joy, and they ran to tell Jesus' disciples.

(9) And look, Jesus met them and said to them, "Hello."[27]

They came up, took hold of his feet, and expressed their adoration.

(10) Then Jesus says to them, "Do not be afraid. Go tell my brothers to go to Galilee, and they will see me there."

Luke 24:9–11

(9) They returned from the tomb and told the eleven[28] and all the others about all these things. (10) The group included Mary Magdalene, Joanna,[29] Mary the mother of James, and the other women with them. They were telling the apostles about these things, (11) but their words sounded like nonsense to them, and they would not believe the women.[30]

MARY MAGDALENE IS THE FIRST TO ENCOUNTER THE RISEN CHRIST

Mark 16:9–11 (longer ending)[31]

(9) After Jesus arose early on Sunday, he appeared first to Mary Magdalene, from whom he had cast out seven demons.[32] (10) She went and told his friends, who were mourning and crying. (11) But when they heard he was alive and had been seen by her, they did not believe it.

John 20:1–18

(1) Early on Sunday morning, while it was still dark, Mary Magdalene comes to the tomb and sees that the stone has been moved away from the tomb. (2) So she runs and comes to Simon Peter and the other disciple, whom Jesus loved,[33] and she says to them, "They have taken the master from the tomb, and we do not know where they have put him."

(3) So Peter and the other disciple went out, and they were on their way to the tomb. (4) The two of them were both running, but the other disciple ran faster than Peter and reached the tomb first. (5) Stooping down, he sees the strips of linen burial cloth lying there, but he did not go in. (6) Simon Peter comes after him, and he went into the tomb. He also sees the

strips of linen cloth lying there, (7) and the cloth that was used to cover the head, lying not with the strips of linen but rolled up by itself. (8) Then the other disciple, who reached the tomb first, went in. He saw and he believed. (9) But they still did not understand the scripture that said he must rise from the dead, (10) and so the disciples went back home.

(11) Mary stood crying outside the tomb. As she was crying, she was stooping to look into the tomb, (12) and she sees two messengers[34] dressed in white and seated where Jesus' body had been, one at the head and the other at the feet.[35]

(13) They ask her, "Woman, why are you crying?"

She answers them, "They have taken my master away, and I do not know where they have put him."

(14) The moment she said this she turned around and sees Jesus standing there, but she did not know it was Jesus.

(15) Jesus asks her, "Woman, why are you crying? Who are you looking for?"

Thinking he was the gardener, she replies to him, "Mister, if you have moved him, tell me where you put him so I can go and get him."

(16) Jesus says to her, "Mary."

She turns around and says to him in Hebrew, "Rabbouni," which means teacher.[36]

(17) Jesus tells her, "Do not touch me,[37] because I have not yet gone back to the father. But go to my brothers and tell them I am going back to my father and your father, to my God and your God."

(18) Mary Magdalene goes and tells the disciples, "I have seen the master," and she relates what he told her.

Additional Stories About Women Around Jesus

THE STORY OF THE WOMAN WHO WAS A SINNER AND WHO ANOINTED JESUS' FEET

Luke 7:36–50

(36) One of the Pharisees invited Jesus to have dinner with him, and he went to the Pharisee's house and reclined at his table. (37) Look, when a woman who was a sinner from that town found out that Jesus was dining at the Pharisee's house, she came by with an alabaster jar of myrrh,[38] (38) and she stood behind him at his feet, weeping. Her tears began to make his feet wet, and so she was wiping them dry with her hair, kissing his feet, and anointing them with myrrh.

(39) The Pharisee who had invited him saw this and said to himself, "If this man were a prophet, he would know who this is who is touching him and what sort of woman she is, for she is a sinner."

(40) Jesus answered and said to him, "Simon,[39] I have something to tell you."

"Teacher, tell me," he said.

(41) "There were two men who owed money to a certain moneylender. One owed five hundred denarii, the other fifty.[40] (42) Since neither of them had the money to pay him back, the lender canceled the debts of both. Now which of them will love him more?"

(43) Simon answered and said, "I suppose the one who had the larger debt canceled."

Jesus said to him, "You are right."

(44) Then he turned toward the woman and said to Simon, "Do you see this woman? I came into your house and you did not offer me water for my feet, but she has washed my feet with her tears and dried them with her hair. (45) You did not offer me a kiss, but this woman, from the time I arrived, has not stopped kissing my feet. (46) You did not anoint my head with oil, but she has anointed my feet with myrrh. (47) For this reason, I tell you, her many sins have been forgiven, for she has loved much. But one who is forgiven little loves little."

(48) Jesus said to her, "Your sins have been forgiven."

(49) Then the other dinner guests began to say among themselves, "Who is this who even forgives sins?"

(50) And he said to the woman, "You faith has saved you. Go in peace."

THE STORY OF THE WOMAN
WHO ANOINTED JESUS AT BETHANY

Mark 14:1–9

(1) Passover and the Feast of Unleavened Bread were only two days away, and the chief priests and scholars were looking for some way to arrest Jesus through trickery and kill him.

(2) "But not during the feast," they said, "or the people may riot."

(3) While he was in Bethany, at the house of Simon the leper,[41] and he was reclining at his table, a woman came in with an alabaster jar of myrrh, made of pure and costly nard. She broke the jar and poured the myrrh on his head.

(4) Some were indignant and said to themselves, "Why has the myrrh been wasted? (5) This myrrh could have been sold for more than three hundred denarii[42] and the money given to the poor." And they were angry with her.

12

(6) But Jesus said, "Leave her alone. Why are you bothering her? She has done a lovely thing to me. (7) You always have the poor around, and you can help them whenever you want, but you will not always have me around. (8) She did what she could. She anointed my body for burial ahead of time. (9) I tell you the truth, wherever the good news is preached throughout the world, what she has done will also be told in memory of her."[43]

THE STORY OF MARY AND MARTHA OF BETHANY

Luke 10:38–42

(38) As Jesus and the disciples were on the way, he came to a village where a woman named Martha welcomed him into her home. (39) She had a sister named Mary, who sat at the master's feet and listened to what he had to say. (40) But Martha was getting distracted by all the serving she had to do. She approached Jesus and said to him, "Master, do you not care that my sister has left me to do all the serving by myself? Tell her that she should help me."

(41) The master answered and said to her, "Martha, Martha, you are worried and upset about many things, (42) but only one thing is necessary. Mary has made the better choice, and it will not be taken away from her."

John 11:1–5

(1) Someone named Lazarus was ill. He was from Bethany, the village of Mary and her sister Martha. (2) This Mary, whose brother Lazarus was ill, was the same person who anointed the master with myrrh and wiped his feet dry with her hair. (3) So the sisters sent for Jesus and said, "Master, the one you love is ill."

(4) When Jesus heard this, he said, "This illness is not fatal. Rather, it is to show God's glory, so that God's son may be glorified through it."

(5) Jesus loved Martha and her sister and Lazarus.

John 11:17–20

(17) When Jesus arrived, he found out that Lazarus had already been in the tomb four days. (18) Bethany was near Jerusalem, about two miles away, (19) and many of the Jews had come to Martha and Mary to comfort them in the loss of their brother. (20) When Martha heard that Jesus was coming, she went to meet him, but Mary stayed at home.

John 11:28–35

(28) After Martha said this, she went to call her sister Mary, and she told her privately, "The teacher is here and is asking for you." (29) When she heard this, she got up quickly and went to him.

(30) Jesus had not yet arrived at the village, but he was still where Martha had met him.

(31) When the Jews, who were with Mary in the house, comforting her, saw her get up quickly and go out, they followed her, thinking she was going to the tomb to mourn there. (32) When Mary got to where Jesus was and saw him, she fell at his feet and said to him, "Master, if you had been here, my brother would not have died."

(33) When Jesus saw her crying, and the Jews who came with her also crying, he was deeply moved in spirit and he was troubled, (34) and he said, "Where have you laid him?"

They say to him, "Master, come and see."

(35) Jesus wept.

John 12:1–8

(1) Six days before Passover Jesus came to Bethany, where Lazarus lived, whom Jesus had raised from the dead. (2) There they prepared a dinner for him. Martha did the serving, and Lazarus was one of those reclining at the table with him.

(3) Mary brought in about a pint of pure and costly nard, anointed Jesus' feet, and wiped his feet dry with her hair, and the house was filled with the fragrance of the myrrh.

(4) Judas Iscariot, the disciple who was going to betray him, says, (5) "Why was this myrrh not sold for three hundred denarii[44] and the money given to the poor?" (6) He did not say this because he cared for the poor but because he was a thief. He was in charge of the money bag, and he would help himself to what was deposited into it.

(7) Jesus said, "Leave her alone. Let her keep it for the day of my burial. (8) You always have the poor around, and you will not always have me around."

❖CHAPTER 2❖

The Gospel of Mary

THE GOSPEL OF MARY is a Gospel known from the Coptic version in a Berlin gnostic codex (Papyrus Berolinensis 8502, the first tractate) and from two Greek fragments (Papyrus Oxyrhynchus 3525 and Papyrus Rylands 463). The Coptic version is the most complete text, but the Coptic Gospel of Mary is missing six manuscript pages at the beginning and four manuscript pages in the middle. Presumably the Gospel of Mary was originally composed in Greek, but the date and place of composition are unknown. Karen King has suggested that the original Gospel of Mary may have been penned in the late first or early second century, perhaps in Syria or Egypt. This suggestion is rather general, but this may be the best estimate that can be offered at this time.

The extant texts of the Gospel of Mary present a dialogue in which the savior (Jesus) discusses various topics with his disciples, particularly Mary (almost certainly Mary Magdalene) and Levi, who understand correctly, and Peter and his brother Andrew, who do not understand and do not accept Mary's teaching. The text begins with a discussion of the nature and destiny of matter, and the savior declares that all creation will return back to the root of its nature. Further, says Jesus, there really is nothing like sin, if sin is thought to be simple wrongdoing. Sin, if we may call it that, is actually cosmic adultery—that is, it is getting improperly connected in the world. Sin in this sense means allowing the good spiritual nature to get mixed up with what is contrary to nature, and such mingling makes people become sick and die.

The savior then goes on, in the Gospel of Mary, to give encouragement and offer peace to the disciples. He advises them not to be distracted by looking here and there, but rather to look within themselves, where the child of humanity (or son of man, as the phrase traditionally has been translated) is to be found. This should be the gospel the disciples preach, not a legalistic set of rules and regulations. And having said this, the savior leaves, in a way that recalls either the crucifixion or the ascension of the savior in other texts. In either case, he is gone.

The disciples are disturbed by the departure of the savior. They fear for their own lives, for if the savior was crucified, they might also be in danger. Mary, however, rises to comfort and assure them. Peter admits that the savior loved Mary more than other women, and so he asks her to recount what the savior told her but not the other disciples. She recalls how she saw the master in a vision—and then, unfortunately, the text breaks off for four pages. When the text resumes, Mary is still rehearsing the vision: as she recounts it, the soul of a person, on its way—or on her way, since the soul is usually personified in ancient literature as being female in gender—to the realm above, is interrogated by the powers of the cosmos, and overcomes the powers and ascends beyond them. In this way the soul in the vision is liberated from passion and ignorance, and returns to the spiritual realm of the divine.

Andrew and Peter appreciate none of this, and Peter doubts the veracity of Mary's teaching. Mary in turn complains bitterly, and Levi comes to Mary's defense, noting that the savior knew and loved Mary. Levi rouses the disciples to put on perfect humanity and go out to preach. In the Rylands papyrus Levi leaves to teach the good news; in the Coptic version (translated in this chapter) the other disciples also proclaim the gospel.

In the Gospel of Mary the words of Mary Magdalene are uttered clearly and profoundly to communicate teaching and revelation. The conflict between Peter and Mary, also well known from the Gospel of Thomas and Pistis Sophia, highlights the central place of Mary Magdalene as beloved disciple of Jesus and preeminent leader in the early church.

———

FOR FURTHER READING: Esther A. de Boer, *The Gospel of Mary*; Karen L. King, *The Gospel of Mary of Magdala*; Karen L. King, "The Gospel of Mary"; Anne Pasquier, *L'Évangile selon Marie*; R. McL. Wilson and George W. MacRae, "The Gospel According to Mary."

The Gospel of Mary[1]

"Will matter be destroyed or not?"[2]

The savior replied, "All natures, all formed things, all creatures exist in and with each other, and they will dissolve into their own root. The nature of matter is dissolved into the root of its nature. Whoever has ears to hear should hear."[3]

Peter said to him, "You have explained everything to us. Tell us also, what is the sin of the world?"

The savior replied, "There is no such thing as sin, but you create sin when you mingle as in adultery,[4] and this is called sin.[5] For this reason the good came among you, to those of every nature, in order to restore nature to its root."

He continued, "That is why you become sick and die, for [you love] (8) what [deceives you].[6] Whoever has a mind should understand.

"Matter gave birth to passion that is without form, because it comes from what is contrary to nature, and then confusion arose in the whole body. That is why I told you, Be of good courage.[7] And if you are discouraged, be encouraged in the presence of the diversity of forms of nature.[8] Whoever has ears to hear should hear."

When the blessed one said this, he greeted all of them and said, "Peace be with you. Receive my peace.[9] Be careful that no one leads you astray by saying, 'Look here' or 'Look there.' The child of humanity[10] is within you.[11] Follow that.[12] Those who seek it will find it. Go and preach the good news of the kingdom. Do not (9) lay down any rules other than what I have given you, and do not establish law, as the lawgiver did, or you will be bound by it."

When he said this, he left them.[13]

MARY CONSOLES THE DISCIPLES, AND PETER CHALLENGES MARY

The disciples were grieved. They wept profoundly and said, "How can we go to the gentiles and preach the good news of the kingdom of the child of humanity? If they did not spare him, how will we be spared?"

Mary[14] stood up, greeted them all,[15] and said to her brothers,[16] "Do not weep or grieve or be in doubt, for his grace will be with you all and will protect you. Rather, let us praise his greatness, for he has prepared us and made us truly human."

When Mary said this, she turned their hearts to the good, and they began to discuss the words of the [savior]. (10)

Peter said to Mary, "Sister, we know the savior loved you more than any other woman.[17] Tell us the words of the savior that you remember, which you know but we do not, because we have not heard them."

Mary answered and said, "What is hidden from you I shall reveal to you."

She began to speak these words to them.

She said, "I saw the master in a vision and I said to him, 'Master, today I saw you in a vision.'[18]

"He answered and said to me, 'Blessings on you, since you did not waver when you saw me. For where the mind is, the treasure is.'[19]

"I said to him, 'Master, how does a person see a vision, with the soul or with the spirit?'

"The savior answered and said, 'A person sees neither with

the soul nor with the spirit. The mind, which is between the two, sees the vision. . . .'"

❋ ❋

MARY RECOUNTS HER VISION OF THE SOUL'S ASCENT

"Desire said, 'I did not see you descending, but now I see you ascending. Why are you lying, since you belong to me?'[20]

"The soul answered and said, 'I saw you, but you did not see me or know me. To you I was only a garment,[21] and you did not recognize me.'

"After the soul said this, she left, rejoicing greatly.

"The soul approached the third power, called ignorance. The power questioned the soul, saying, 'Where are you going? You are bound by wickedness, you are bound, so do not pass judgment.'

"The soul said, 'Why do you pass judgment on me, though I have not passed judgment? I was bound, but I have not bound. I was not recognized, but I have recognized that all is to be dissolved, both what is earthly (16) and what is heavenly.'

"When the soul overcame the third power, she ascended and saw the fourth power. It took seven forms:

The first form is darkness,
the second, desire,
the third, ignorance,
the fourth, death wish,
the fifth, fleshly kingdom,
the sixth, foolish fleshly wisdom,
the seventh, angry person's wisdom.

"These are the seven powers of wrath.[22]

"The powers asked the soul, 'Where are you coming from, slayer of humans, and where are you going, destroyer of realms?'

"The soul answered and said, 'What binds me is slain, what

surrounds me is destroyed, my desire is gone, ignorance is dead. In a world I was freed (17) through[23] another world, and in an image I was freed through a heavenly image. The fetter of forgetfulness is temporary. From now on I shall rest, through the course of the time of the age, in silence.'"

PETER AND ANDREW DOUBT MARY'S WORD

When Mary said this, she became silent, since the savior had spoken this much to her.

Andrew answered and said to the brothers, "Say what you think about what she said, but I do not believe the savior said this. These teachings certainly are strange ideas."

Peter voiced similar concerns. He asked the others about the savior: "Did he really speak with a woman in private, without our knowledge? Should we all turn and listen to her? Did he prefer her to us?"[24] (18)

LEVI SPEAKS ON BEHALF OF MARY

Then Mary wept and said to Peter, "My brother Peter, what do you think? Do you think that I made this up by myself or that I am lying about the savior?"

Levi[25] answered and said to Peter, "Peter, you always are angry. Now I see you arguing against this woman like an adversary. If the savior made her worthy, who are you to reject her? Surely the savior knows her well. That is why he has loved her more than us.[26]

"So, we should be ashamed and put on perfect humanity and acquire[27] it, as he commanded us, and preach the good news, not making any rule or law other than what the savior indicated."

When (19) [Levi said] this, they[28] began to leave [in order to] teach and preach.

CHAPTER 3

The Gospel of Thomas

THE GOSPEL OF THOMAS is a collection of 114 sayings of Jesus—
"hidden sayings that the living Jesus spoke and Judas Thomas the
Twin recorded." The Gospel of Thomas is the second tractate of
codex 2 of the Nag Hammadi library, where it is preserved in
Coptic translation. Three Greek fragments of the Gospel of
Thomas also survive (Papyrus Oxyrhynchus 1, 654, and 655), as
well as testimonies in early Christian literature, especially Hippolytus of Rome. Most likely the Gospel of Thomas was composed in Greek, probably in Syria, perhaps at Edessa, where
Thomas was revered and his bones venerated. A reasonable case
can be made for a first-century date for a first edition of the
Gospel of Thomas.

According to saying 1 of the Gospel of Thomas, "Whoever discovers the interpretation of these sayings will not taste death." The
Gospel of Thomas does not proclaim a gospel of the cross, as do the
Gospels of Mark, Matthew, Luke, John, and Peter, but rather a gospel
of wisdom, and hearers and readers are encouraged to encounter
the sayings, interact with them, and discover for themselves their

interpretation and meaning. And according to the Gospel of Thomas, that is how people attain salvation and life.

Among the sayings in the Gospel of Thomas, two refer to a woman named Mary. In saying 21 the question of a person named Mary ("What are your disciples like?") prompts Jesus to offer words about life, trouble, and the consummation of things in the world. While Mary here may be Mary Magdalene, there is nothing to confirm—or to deny—such an identification. In saying 114 Mary comes into conflict with Peter, and this Mary is almost certainly Mary Magdalene. In a similar fashion Mary Magdalene faces the hostility of Peter in the Gospel of Mary and Pistis Sophia, and in all these texts Mary finally is vindicated.

Gospel of Thomas saying 114 has Jesus declare that Mary can be saved when she becomes male, "for every female who makes herself male will enter heaven's kingdom." At first glance it may appear that Peter, not Mary, is the one who is vindicated here. After all, Mary must become male to be saved, and that could suggest Peter was right all along. To be sure, there are a variety of ways in which the female becoming male has been interpreted in theory and in practice. For example, in the Acts of Philip (discussed earlier, in the general introduction), Jesus is made to praise Mary (understood by François Bovon to be Mary Magdalene) for her courageous, masculine spirit, and he advises her to avoid dressing like a woman and instead to wear male clothing. The best interpretation of the female becoming male here in the Gospel of Thomas, however, seems to involve a symbolic understanding. Commonly in the world of antiquity the female is made to symbolize what is earthly and perishable and the male what is heavenly and imperishable. If that is also the case here, then the transformation of the female into the male impacts all people, women and men, who seek to leave what is perishable and attain what is imperishable. Then what is true for Mary becoming male is true for all people, whatever their gender, who participate in femaleness. The world of perishability is overcome, the dying cosmos of the mother goddess is transcended, and she—and all human beings who are physical and earthly—can be transformed to the spiritual and heavenly.

––––––––

FOR FURTHER READING: Marvin Meyer, *The Gospel of Thomas;* Marvin Meyer, *Secret Gospels;* Elaine H. Pagels, *Beyond Belief;* Stephen J. Patterson, *The Gospel of Thomas and Jesus;* Stephen J. Patterson, James M. Robinson, and Hans-Gebhard Bethge, *The Fifth Gospel;* Richard Valantasis, *The Gospel of Thomas.*

The Gospel of Thomas[1]

PROLOGUE

These are the hidden sayings that the living Jesus spoke and Judas Thomas the Twin[2] recorded.[3]

(1) And he[4] said, "Whoever discovers the interpretation of these sayings will not taste death."[5]

(2) Jesus said, "Let one who seeks not stop seeking until one finds. When one finds, one will be troubled. When one is troubled, one will marvel and will reign over all."[6]

(3) Jesus said, "If your leaders say to you, 'Look, the kingdom is in heaven,' then the birds of heaven will precede you. If they say to you, 'It is in the sea,'[7] then the fish will precede you. Rather, the kingdom is inside you and it is outside you.[8]

"When you know yourselves, then you will be known, and you will understand that you are children of the living father. But if you do not know yourselves, then you dwell in poverty, and you are poverty."[9]

(4) Jesus said, "The person old in days will not hesitate to ask a little child seven days old[10] about the place of life, and that person will live.[11] For many of the first will be last[12] and will become a single one."

(5) Jesus said, "Know what is in front of your face, and what is hidden from you will be disclosed to you.[13] For there is nothing hidden that will not be revealed."[14]

(6) His disciples asked him and said to him, "Do you want us to fast? How should we pray? Should we give to charity? What diet should we observe?"[15]

Jesus said, "Do not lie, and do not do what you hate,[16] because all things are disclosed before heaven.[17] For there is nothing hidden that will not be revealed, and there is nothing covered that will remain undisclosed."[18]

(7) Jesus said, "Blessings on the lion that the human will eat, so that the lion becomes human. And cursed[19] is the human that the lion will eat, and the lion will become human."[20]

(8) And he said, "Humankind[21] is like a wise fisherman who cast his net into the sea and drew it up from the sea full of little fish. Among them the wise fisherman discovered a fine large fish. He threw all the little fish back into the sea and with no difficulty chose the large fish. Whoever has ears to hear should hear."[22]

(9) Jesus said, "Look, the sower went out, took a handful of seeds, and scattered them. Some fell on the road, and the birds came and pecked them up. Others fell on rock, and they did not take root in the soil and did not produce heads of grain. Others fell on thorns, and they choked the seeds and worms devoured them. And others fell on good soil, and it brought forth a good crop. It yielded sixty per measure and one hundred twenty per measure."[23]

(10) Jesus said, "I have thrown fire upon the world, and look, I am watching it until it blazes."[24]

(11) Jesus said, "This heaven will pass away, and the one above it will pass away.[25]

"The dead are not alive, and the living will not die.

"During the days when you ate what is dead, you made it alive. When you are in the light, what will you do?[26]

"On the day when you were one, you became two. But when you become two, what will you do?"

(12) The disciples said to Jesus, "We know that you are going to leave us. Who will be our leader?"

Jesus said to them, "No matter where you have come from, you are to go to James the Just, for whose sake heaven and earth came into being."

(13) Jesus said to his disciples, "Compare me to something and tell me what I am like."

Simon Peter said to him, "You are like a just messenger."[27]

Matthew said to him, "You are like a wise philosopher."

Thomas said to him, "Teacher, my mouth is utterly unable to say what you are like."

Jesus said, "I am not your teacher. Because you have drunk, you have become intoxicated from the bubbling spring that I have tended."

And he took him, and withdrew, and spoke three sayings[28] to him.

When Thomas came back to his friends, they asked him, "What did Jesus say to you?"

Thomas said to them, "If I tell you one of the sayings he spoke to me, you will pick up rocks and stone me, and fire will come from the rocks and consume you."[29]

(14) Jesus said to them, "If you fast, you will bring sin upon yourselves, and if you pray, you will be condemned, and if you give to charity, you will harm your spirits.[30]

"When you go into any region and walk through the countryside,[31] when people receive you, eat what they serve you and heal the sick among them.[32] For what goes into your mouth will not defile you; rather, it is what comes out of your mouth that will defile you."[33]

(15) Jesus said, "When you see one who was not born of woman, fall on your faces and worship. That is your father."[34]

(16) Jesus said, "Perhaps people think that I have come to impose peace upon the world. They do not know that I have come to impose conflicts upon the earth: fire, sword, war. For there will be five in a house: there will be three against two and two against three, father against son and son against father, and they will stand alone."[35]

(17) Jesus said, "I shall give you what no eye has seen, what

no ear has heard, what no hand has touched, what has not arisen in the human heart."[36]

(18) The disciples said to Jesus, "Tell us how our end will be."[37]

Jesus said, "Have you discovered the beginning, then, so that you are seeking the end? For where the beginning is the end will be. Blessings on one who stands at the beginning: That one will know the end and will not taste death."[38]

(19) Jesus said, "Blessings on one who came into being before coming into being.[39]

"If you become my disciples and listen to my sayings, these stones will serve you.[40]

"For there are five trees in paradise for you; they do not change, summer or winter, and their leaves do not fall. Whoever knows them will not taste death."[41]

(20) The disciples said to Jesus, "Tell us what heaven's kingdom is like."

He said to them, "It is like a mustard seed. <It> is the smallest of all seeds, but when it falls on prepared soil, it produces a large plant and becomes a shelter for birds of heaven."[42]

(21) Mary[43] said to Jesus, "What are your disciples like?"

He said, "They are like children living in a field that is not theirs.[44] When the owners of the field come, they will say, 'Give our field back to us.' They take off their clothes in front of them in order to give it back to them, and they return their field to them.[45]

"For this reason I say, if the owner of a house knows that a thief is coming, he will be on guard before the thief arrives and will not let the thief break into the house of his estate and steal his possessions.[46] As for you, then, be on guard against the world. Arm yourselves with great strength, or the robbers might find a way to get to you, for the trouble you expect will come. Let there be among you a person who understands.

"When the crop ripened, the person came quickly with sickle in hand and harvested it.[47] Whoever has ears to hear should hear."

(22) Jesus saw some babies nursing. He said to his disciples, "These nursing babies are like those who enter the kingdom."

They said to him, "Then shall we enter the kingdom as babies?"

Jesus said to them, "When you make the two into one, and when you make the inner like the outer and the outer like the inner, and the upper like the lower, and when you make male and female into a single one, so that the male will not be male nor the female be female, when you make eyes in place of an eye, a hand in place of a hand, a foot in place of a foot, an image in place of an image, then you will enter [the kingdom]."[48]

❊ ❊

(50) Jesus said, "If they say to you, 'Where have you come from?' say to them, 'We have come from the light, from the place where the light came into being by itself, established [itself], and appeared in their image.' If they say to you, 'Is it you?' say, 'We are its children, and we are the chosen of the living father.' If they ask you, 'What is the evidence of your father in you?' say to them, 'It is motion and rest.'"[49]

(51) His disciples said to him, "When will the rest for the dead take place, and when will the new world come?"

He said to them, "What you look for has come, but you do not know it."[50]

(52) His disciples said to him, "Twenty-four prophets[51] have spoken in Israel, and they all spoke of you."

He said to them, "You have disregarded the living one who is in your presence and have spoken of the dead."[52]

(53) His disciples said to him, "Is circumcision useful or not?"

He said to them, "If it were useful, children's fathers would produce them already circumcised from their mothers. Rather, the true circumcision in spirit has become valuable in every respect."[53]

(54) Jesus said, "Blessings on the poor, for yours is heaven's kingdom."[54]

(55) Jesus said, "Whoever does not hate father and mother cannot be a disciple of me, and whoever does not hate brothers and sisters and bear the cross as I do will not be worthy of me."[55]

❋ ❋

(61) Jesus said, "Two will rest on a couch; one will die, one will live."[56]

Salome[57] said, "Who are you, mister? You have climbed onto my couch[58] and eaten from my table as if you are from someone."[59]

Jesus said to her, "I am the one who comes from what is whole. I was given from the things of my father."[60]

"I am your disciple."[61]

"For this reason I say, if one is <whole>, one will be filled with light,[62] but if one is divided, one will be filled with darkness."

❋ ❋

(73) Jesus said, "The harvest is large but the workers are few. So beg the master to send out workers to the harvest."[63]

(74) Someone said,[64] "Master, there are many around the drinking trough,[65] but there is nothing[66] in the well."

(75) Jesus said, "There are many standing at the door, but those who are alone will enter the wedding chamber."[67]

(76) Jesus said, "The father's kingdom is like a merchant who had a supply of merchandise and then found a pearl. That merchant was prudent; he sold the merchandise and bought the single pearl for himself.[68] So also with you, seek his treasure that is unfailing, that is enduring, where no moth comes to devour and no worm destroys."[69]

(77) Jesus said, "I am the light that is over all things.[70] I am all. From me all has come forth, and to me all has reached.[71] Split a piece of wood; I am there. Lift up the stone, and you will find me there."[72]

(78) Jesus said, "Why have you come out to the countryside? To see a reed shaken by the wind? And to see a person dressed in soft clothes, [like your] rulers and your powerful ones? They are dressed in soft clothes, and they cannot understand truth."[73]

(79) A woman in the crowd said to him, "Blessings on the womb that bore you and the breasts that fed you."[74]

He said to [her], "Blessings on those who have heard the word of the father and have truly kept it.[75] For there will be days when you will say, 'Blessings on the womb that has not conceived and the breasts that have not given milk.'"[76]

(80) Jesus said, "Whoever has come to know the world has discovered the body, and whoever has discovered the body, of that person the world is not worthy."[77]

(81) Jesus said, "Let one who has become wealthy reign, and let one who has power renounce it."[78]

(82) Jesus said, "Whoever is near me is near the fire, and whoever is far from me is far from the kingdom."[79]

(83) Jesus said, "Images are visible to people, but the light within them is hidden in the image of the father's light. He will be disclosed, but his image is hidden by his light."

(84) Jesus said, "When you see your likeness, you are happy. But when you see your images that came into being before you and that neither die nor become visible, how much you will bear!"[80]

(85) Jesus said, "Adam came from great power[81] and great wealth, but he was not worthy of you. For had he been worthy, [he would] not [have tasted] death."

(86) Jesus said, "[Foxes have] their dens and birds have their nests, but the child of humanity has no place to lay his head and rest."[82]

(87) Jesus said, "How miserable is the body that depends on a body, and how miserable is the soul that depends on these two."[83]

(88) Jesus said, "The messengers[84] and the prophets will

come to you and give you what is yours. You, in turn, give them what you have, and say to yourselves, 'When will they come and take what is theirs?'"[85]

(89) Jesus said, "Why do you wash the outside of the cup? Do you not understand that the one who made the inside is also the one who made the outside?"[86]

(90) Jesus said, "Come to me, for my yoke is easy and my mastery is gentle, and you will find rest for yourselves."[87]

(91) They said to him, "Tell us who you are so that we may believe in you."

He said to them, "You examine the face of heaven and earth, but you have not come to know the one who is in your presence, and you do not know how to examine this moment."[88]

(92) Jesus said, "Seek and you will find.[89] In the past, however, I did not tell you the things about which you asked me then. Now I am willing to tell them, but you are not seeking them.[90]

(93) "Do not give what is holy to dogs, or they might throw them upon the manure pile. Do not throw pearls [to] swine, or they might make [mud] of it."[91]

(94) Jesus [said], "One who seeks will find; for [one who knocks] it will be opened."[92]

(95) [Jesus said], "If you have money, do not lend it at interest. Rather, give [it] to someone from whom you will not get it back."[93]

(96) Jesus [said], "The father's kingdom is like [a] woman. She took a little yeast, [hid] it in dough, and made it into large loaves of bread. Whoever has ears should hear."[94]

(97) Jesus said, "The [father's] kingdom is like a woman who was carrying a [jar] full of meal. While she was walking along [a] distant road, the handle of the jar broke and the meal spilled behind her [along] the road. She did not know it; she had not noticed a problem. When she reached her house, she put the jar down and discovered that it was empty."[95]

(98) Jesus said, "The father's kingdom is like a person who wanted to put someone powerful to death. While at home he drew his sword and thrust it into the wall to find out whether his hand would go in. Then he killed the powerful one."[96]

(99) The disciples said to him, "Your brothers and your mother are standing outside."

He said to them, "Those here who do the will of my father are my brothers and my mother. They are the ones who will enter my father's kingdom."[97]

(100) They showed Jesus a gold coin and said to him, "Caesar's people demand taxes from us."

He said to them, "Give Caesar the things that are Caesar's, give God the things that are God's, and give me what is mine.[98]

(101) "Whoever does not hate [father] and mother as I do cannot be a [disciple] of me, and whoever does [not] love [father and] mother as I do cannot be a [disciple of] me. For my mother [gave me falsehood],[99] but my true [mother][100] gave me life."[101]

(102) Jesus said, "Shame on the Pharisees, for they are like a dog sleeping in the cattle manger, for it does not eat or [let] the cattle eat."[102]

(103) Jesus said, "Blessings on the person who knows at what point the robbers are going to enter, so that [he] may arise, bring together his estate, and arm himself before they enter."[103]

(104) They said to Jesus, "Come, let us pray today and let us fast."

Jesus said, "What sin have I committed, or how have I been undone? Rather, when the bridegroom leaves the wedding chamber, then let people fast and pray."[104]

(105) Jesus said, "Whoever knows the father and the mother will be called the child of a whore."[105]

(106) Jesus said, "When you make the two into one, you will become children of humanity, and when you say, 'Mountain, move from here,' it will move."[106]

(107) Jesus said, "The kingdom is like a shepherd who had a hundred sheep. One of them, the largest, went astray. He left the ninety-nine and sought the one until he found it. After he had gone to this trouble, he said to the sheep, 'I love you more than the ninety-nine.'"[107]

(108) Jesus said, "Whoever drinks from my mouth will become like me; I myself shall become that person, and the hidden things will be revealed to that person."[108]

(109) Jesus said, "The kingdom is like a person who had a treasure hidden in his field but did not know it. And [when] he died, he left it to his [son]. The son [did] not know about it. He took over the field and sold it. The buyer went plowing, [discovered] the treasure, and began to lend money at interest to whomever he wished."[109]

(110) Jesus said, "Let someone who has found the world and has become wealthy renounce the world."[110]

(111) Jesus said, "The heavens and the earth will roll up in your presence, and whoever is living from the living one will not see death."[111]

Does not Jesus say, "Whoever has found oneself, of that person the world is not worthy"?[112]

(112) Jesus said, "Shame on the flesh that depends on the soul. Shame on the soul that depends on the flesh."[113]

(113) His disciples said to him, "When will the kingdom come?"

"It will not come by watching for it. It will not be said,[114] 'Look, here it is,' or 'Look, there it is.' Rather, the father's kingdom is spread out upon the earth, and people do not see it."[115]

(114) Simon Peter said to them, "Mary should leave us, for females are not worthy of life."

Jesus said, "Look, I shall guide her to make her male, so that she too may become a living spirit resembling you males. For every female who makes herself male will enter heaven's kingdom."[116]

CHAPTER 4

The Gospel of Philip

THE GOSPEL OF PHILIP is a gnostic anthology with a long series of meditations written by disciples of Valentinus, the brilliant second-century mystic, teacher, and preacher who flourished in Alexandria and Rome and was reputed to be a candidate for the position of bishop of Rome—or, as we would say today, the position of pope of the Roman church. Valentinus may have been the author of the Gospel of Truth, a beautiful gnostic sermon preserved among the Nag Hammadi texts. Bentley Layton suggests that some of the excerpts in the Gospel of Philip could also conceivably come from Valentinus. The Gospel of Philip is the third tractate in codex 2 of the Nag Hammadi library, and it is copied immediately after the Gospel of Thomas. Whether the text was composed in Syria during the second century or a bit later, as has been proposed, remains somewhat uncertain, though the references to Syriac terms suggest an acquaintance with Syriac language and literature.

In the selections from the Gospel of Philip given here, Mary Magdalene is mentioned only twice, but the passages are noteworthy. It is said in the Gospel of Philip 59 that three women always walked with Jesus, and all three were named Mary: Mary his mother, a sister of Jesus (or perhaps a sister of the mother of Jesus—the Coptic text is ambiguous and seems to need emendation), and Mary Magdalene. Mary Magdalene is called his companion, partner, or consort (*koinônos*, a word of Greek origin, and *hôtre*, a word of Egyptian origin). Later, in the Gospel of Philip 63–64, it is said that Jesus loved Mary Magdalene more than he loved the other disciples and kissed her often—perhaps on her mouth, but the Coptic text requires restoration here in order to specify precisely where on Mary Jesus placed his kisses. In the critical edition edited by Bentley Layton, the feet, a cheek, and the forehead of Mary are also raised as possible objects of kisses.

Loving and kissing are also discussed elsewhere in the Gospel of Philip. Sexuality, marriage, and the bridal chamber are familiar themes in the gospel, and while sex is accepted and marriage is judged to be necessary ("[Without] it, the world would [not] exist"), the sacramental mystery of the bridal chamber is emphasized. The place of sexuality and marriage in the Gospel of Philip and other Valentinian texts has been debated by scholars, and some have emphasized a more physical and others a more spiritual understanding of marriage among Valentinians. In any case, according to the Gospel of Philip, the sacramental bridal chamber is pure and enlightened, is a matter of will, and leads to the union, the spiritual union, of the partners. Ultimately the bridal chamber leads to a union that has implications for this world and the next, and as a result, the bridal chamber may be considered the greatest of the sacraments. Nonetheless, truth is embraced in symbols and images, and the truth of the bridal chamber likewise comes through symbols and images.

The Gospel of Philip also acknowledges the role of kissing. The text states, "The perfect conceive and give birth through a kiss."

This wording may connote a ceremonial kiss, or it may designate how life or spirit is communicated. It may also be connected to sexual intercourse.

Hence, in her study of sexuality and marriage in the Gospel of Philip and among Valentinians in general, April D. DeConick concludes, "Sexual intercourse between Valentinian spouses was to continue until the last spiritual seed was embodied and harvested. On that great day, the Bridal Chamber would open and their spirits would reunite with God. How important was sex to the Valentinians? The coming of the final day and the redemption of God depended on it" (342).

FOR FURTHER READING: Willis Barnstone and Marvin Meyer, *The Gnostic Bible*; April D. DeConick, "The Great Mystery of Marriage"; Bentley Layton, *The Gnostic Scriptures*, 325–53; Bentley Layton, ed., *Nag Hammadi Codex II,2–7*, 1:129–217; Jacques É. Ménard, *L'Évangile selon Philippe*; Kurt Rudolph, *Gnosis*; Hans-Martin Schenke, "Das Evangelium nach Philippus"; Hans-Martin Schenke, "The Gospel of Philip."

The Gospel of Philip[1]

CONVERTS

A Hebrew makes a Hebrew, and such a person is called a convert. A convert does not make a convert. [Some people] are as they [are] and make others [like them], while others (52) simply are.

INHERITING THE LIVING AND THE DEAD

A slave seeks only to be free and does not seek the master's estate.

For a child it is not enough to be a child, but a child claims the father's inheritance.

Heirs to the dead are dead, and what they inherit is dead. Heirs to the living are alive, and they inherit both the living and the dead. The dead inherit nothing, for how could a dead person inherit? If a dead person inherits the living, the living will not die and the dead will come to life.[2]

JESUS, GENTILES, CHRISTIANS

A gentile does not die, never having been alive so as to die. One who has believed in truth is alive, but this person is at risk of dying just by being alive.

Since Christ came, the world has been created, cities have been beautified, and the dead have been buried.

When we were Hebrews we were orphans, with only a mother, but when we became Christians we had a father and a mother.[3]

SOWING AND REAPING

Whoever sows in winter reaps in summer. Winter is the world, summer is the other, eternal realm. Let us sow in the world to reap in summer. And for this reason we should not pray in winter.[4]

From winter comes summer. If someone reaps in winter, the person will not really reap but will pull out the young plants, and such do not produce a crop. [That person's field] is barren not only [now] but also on the Sabbath.[5]

CHRIST CAME

Christ came (53) to purchase some, to save some, to redeem some. He purchased strangers and made them his own, and he brought back his own whom he had laid down of his own will as a deposit. Not only when he appeared did he lay down the soul of his own will as a deposit, but from the beginning of the world he laid down the soul, for the proper moment, according to his will. Then he came forth to take it back, since it had been laid down as a deposit. It had fallen into the hands of robbers and had been stolen, but he saved it. And he redeemed the good in the world and the bad.

LIGHT AND DARKNESS

Light and darkness, life and death, right and left, are siblings[6] of one another, and inseparable. For this reason the good are not good, the bad are not bad, life is not life, death is not death. Each will dissolve into its original nature, but what is superior to the world cannot be dissolved, for it is eternal.[7]

WORDS AND NAMES

The names of worldly things are utterly deceptive, for they turn the heart from what is real to what is unreal. Whoever hears the word *god* thinks not of what is real but rather of what is unreal. So also with the words *father, son, holy spirit, life, light, resurrection, church,* and all the rest, people do not think of what is real but of what is unreal, [though] the words refer to what is real. The words [that are] heard belong to this world. [Do not be] (54) deceived. If words belonged to the eternal realm, they would never be pronounced in this world, nor would they designate worldly things. They would refer to what is in the eternal realm.

THE NAME OF THE FATHER

Only one name is not pronounced in the world, the name the father gave the son. It is the name above all; it is the father's name. For the son would not have become father if he had not put on the father's name. Those who have this name understand it but do not speak it. Those who do not have it cannot even understand it.

TRUTH BROUGHT FORTH NAMES

Truth brought forth names[8] in the world for us, and no one can refer to truth without names. Truth is one and many, for us, to teach us about the one, in love, through the many.

THE RULERS

The rulers wanted to fool people, since they saw that people have a kinship with what is truly good. They took the names of the good and assigned them to what is not good, to fool people with names and link the names to what is not good. So, as if they are doing people a favor, they take names from what is not good and transfer them to the good, in their own way of thinking. For they wished to take free people and enslave them forever.

THE FORCES

There are forces[9] that do [favors] for people. They do not want people to come to [salvation], but they want their own existence to continue. For if people come to salvation, sacrifice will [stop] . . . and animals will not be offered up (55) to the forces. In fact, those to whom sacrifices were made were animals.[10] The animals were offered up alive, and after being offered they died. But a human being[11] was offered up to God dead, and the human being came alive.

CHRIST BROUGHT BREAD

Before Christ came there was no bread in the world, just as paradise, where Adam lived, had many trees for animal food but no wheat for human food, and people ate like animals. But when Christ, the perfect human, came, he brought bread from heaven,[12] that humans might be fed with human food.

THE RULERS AND THE HOLY SPIRIT

The rulers thought they did all they did by their own power and will, but the holy spirit was secretly accomplishing all[13] through them by the spirit's will.

SOWING AND REAPING TRUTH

Truth, which has existed from the beginning, is sown everywhere, and many see it being sown but few see it being reaped.

Mary the Mother of Jesus Conceiving

Some said Mary became pregnant by the holy spirit.[14] They are wrong and do not know what they are saying. When did a woman ever get pregnant by a woman?[15]

Mary is the virgin whom none of the powers defiled. This is greatly repugnant to the Hebrews, who are the apostles and apostolic persons. This virgin whom none of the powers defiled [wishes that] the powers would defile themselves.

My Father

The master [would] not have said, "My [father who is] in heaven,"[16] if [he] did not also have another father. He would simply have said, "[My father]."

Take from Every House

The master said to the disciples, "[Take something] (56) from every house and bring it to the father's house, but do not steal while in the father's house and take something away."

❊ ❊

Children of the Perfect Human

The heavenly person has more children than the earthly person. If the children of Adam are numerous but die, how much more numerous are the children of the perfect human, who do not die but are continually being born.

A father produces children, but a child cannot produce children. One who has just been born cannot be a parent. Rather, a child gets brothers and sisters,[17] not children.

All who are born in the world are born of nature, and the others [are nourished] from where they are born. People [are] nourished from the promise of the heavenly place. [If they would be] . . . from the mouth, from which the word comes, (59) they would be nourished from the mouth and would be perfect.

The perfect conceive and give birth through a kiss. That is why we also kiss each other. We conceive from the grace within each other.

THREE WOMEN NAMED MARY

Three women always walked with the master: Mary his mother, <his> sister,[18] and Mary Magdalene, who is called his companion. For "Mary" is the name of his sister, his mother, and his companion.[19]

FATHER, SON, HOLY SPIRIT

Father and *son* are simple names; *holy spirit* is a double name. They[20] are everywhere, above and below, in the hidden and in the visible. The holy spirit is in the visible, and then it is below, and the holy spirit is in the hidden, and then it is above.

HOLY SPIRIT AND EVIL FORCES

Evil forces serve the saints, for they have been blinded by the holy spirit into thinking they are helping their own people when they really are helping the saints.

So a disciple once asked the master for something from the world, and he said, "Ask your mother, and she will give you something from another realm."

WISDOM AND SALT

The apostles said to the disciples, "May our entire offering be provided with salt." For they called [wisdom[21]] salt. Without it an offering is unacceptable.[22] Wisdom is barren, [with no] children, and so she is called [the pillar] of salt.[23] Whenever . . . the holy spirit . . . , (60) and she has many children.

FATHER AND CHILD

A father's possessions belong to his child. As long as the child is young, the child will not have what belongs to it. When the child grows up, the father will turn over all the possessions.

THE LOST

Those who have gone astray are offspring of the spirit, and they go astray because of the spirit. Thus from one spirit the fire blazes and the fire is extinguished.

WISDOM AND WISDOM OF DEATH

There is Echamoth and there is Echmoth. Echamoth is simply wisdom, but Echmoth is the wisdom of death—that is, the wisdom that knows death, that is called little wisdom.[24]

TAME AND WILD ANIMALS

Some animals are tame, such as the bull, the donkey, and the like, while others are wild and live off in the wild. People plow fields with tame animals, and as a result people are nourished, together with animals, whether tame or wild.

So also the perfect human plows with powers that are tame and prepares everything to come into being. Thus the whole place has stability, good and evil, right and left. The holy spirit tends everything and rules over [all] the powers, whether tame or wild and running loose. For the spirit is [resolved] to corral them, so that they cannot escape even if [they] wish.

ADAM AND CAIN

[The one] created[25] was [noble, and you would] expect his children to be (61) noble. If he had not been created but rather had been conceived, you would expect his offspring to be noble. But in fact he was created, and then he produced offspring.

And what nobility this is! First came adultery, then murder. One[26] was born of adultery, for he was the son of the serpent.[27] He became a murderer, like his father, and he killed his brother.[28] Every act of sexual intercourse between those unlike each other is adultery.[29]

GOD THE DYER

God is a dyer. Just as the good dyes, said to be genuine dyes, dissolve into what is dyed in them, so also those whom God dyes become immortal through his colors, for his dyes are immortal. And God dips[30] those to be dipped[31] in water.[32]

SEEING

People cannot see anything that really is without becoming like it. It is not so with people in the world, who see the sun without becoming the sun and see the sky and earth and everything else without becoming them.

Rather, in the realm of truth,
you have seen things there and have become those things,
you have seen the spirit and have become spirit,

you have seen Christ and have become Christ,
you have seen the [father] and will become father.[33]

[Here] in the world you see everything but do not [see] yourself, but there in that realm you see yourself, and you will [become] what you see.

FAITH AND LOVE

Faith receives, love gives. [No one can (62) receive] without faith, and no one can give without love. So to receive we have faith and to love we give. If someone gives without love, that person gets no benefit from what was given.[34]

Anyone who receives something but does not receive the master is still a Hebrew.

JESUS' NAMES

The apostles who came before us used the names *Iesous nazo-raios messias,* which means "Jesus the Nazorean, the Christ."[35] The last name is "Christ," the first name is "Jesus," the middle name is "the Nazarene."[36] *Messias* has two meanings: "Christ"[37] and "measured."[38] In Hebrew *Jesus* means "redemption."[39] *Nazara* means "truth," and so "the Nazarene" means "truth."[40] "Christ" has been "measured"; thus "the Nazarene" and "Jesus"[41] have been measured out.

A PEARL IN MUD

If a pearl is thrown into mud, it will not lose its value, and if it is anointed with balsam, it will not increase its value. It is always precious in its owner's eyes. Likewise, the children of God are precious in the eyes of the father, whatever their circumstances of life.

THE NAME "CHRISTIAN"

If you say, "I am a Jew," no one will be moved. If you say, "I am a Roman," no one will be disturbed. If you say, "I am a Greek, barbarian, slave, free," no one will be troubled. If you say, "I am a Christian," the [world] will be shaken. May I [receive the one] whose name the [world] cannot bear to hear.

GOD IS A MAN-EATER

God is a man-eater, (63) and so people are [sacrificed] to him. Before people were sacrificed, animals were sacrificed, because those to whom they were sacrificed were not gods.

GLASS AND CERAMIC VESSELS

Glass and ceramic vessels are both made with fire. If glass vessels break, they are redone, since they have been made through breath.[42] But if ceramic vessels break, they are destroyed, since they have been made without breath.

A DONKEY TURNING A MILLSTONE

A donkey turning a millstone walked a hundred miles. When it was set loose, it found itself in the same place. Some people travel long distances but get nowhere. By nightfall they have seen no cities or villages, nothing man-made or natural, no powers or angels. These miserable people have labored in vain.

THE EUCHARIST AND JESUS

The eucharist is Jesus. In Syriac it is called *pharisatha*, which means, "that which is spread out." For Jesus came to crucify[43] the world.

THE DYE WORKS OF LEVI

The master went into the dye works of Levi, took seventy-two colored cloths,[44] and threw them into a vat. He drew them out and they all were white. He said, "So the child of humanity has come as a dyer."[45]

WISDOM AND MARY MAGDALENE

Wisdom,[46] who is called barren, is the mother of the angels.

The companion of the [savior] is Mary Magdalene. The [savior loved] her[47] more than [all] the disciples, [and he] kissed her often on her [mouth].[48]

The other [disciples] (64) . . . said to him, "Why do you love her more than all of us?"

The savior answered and said to them, "Why do I not love you like her? If a blind person and one who can see are both in darkness, they are the same. When the light comes, one who can see will see the light, and the blind person will stay in darkness."[49]

ONE WHO IS

The master said, "Blessings on one who is before coming into being. For whoever is, was, and will be."[50]

HUMAN BEINGS AND ANIMALS

The superiority of human beings is not apparent to the eye but lies in what is hidden. Consequently, they are dominant over animals that are stronger than they are and greater in ways apparent and hidden. So animals survive. But when human beings leave them, animals kill and devour each other. Animals have eaten each other because they have found no other food. Now, however, they have food, because humans till the ground.

GOING DOWN INTO THE WATER

Anyone who goes down into the water[51] and comes up without having received anything and says, "I am a Christian," has borrowed the name. But one who receives the holy spirit has the name as a gift. A gift does not have to be paid back, but what is borrowed must be paid. This is how it is with us, when one of us experiences a mystery.

MARRIAGE

The mystery of marriage is great. [Without] it, the world would [not] exist. The existence of [the world depends on] people, and the existence [of people depends on] marriage. Then think of the power of [pure] intercourse, though its image (65) is defiled.

✳ ✳

TRUTH AND NAKEDNESS

Truth did not come into the world naked but in symbols and images. The world cannot receive truth in any other way. There is rebirth and an image of rebirth, and it is by means of this image that one must be reborn. What image is this? It is resurrection. Image must arise through image. By means of this image the bridal chamber[52] and the image must approach the truth. This is restoration.

Those who receive the name of the father, son, and holy spirit and have accepted them must do this. If someone does not accept them, the name[53] will also be taken from that person.

A person receives them in the chrism with the oil of the power of the cross. The apostles called this power the right and the left. This person is no longer a Christian but is Christ.

SACRAMENTS

The master [did] everything in a mystery: baptism, chrism, eucharist, redemption, and bridal chamber.

THE INNER AND THE OUTER

[For this reason] he[54] said, "I have come to make [the lower] like the [upper and the] outer like the [inner, and to unite] them in that place."[55] [He spoke] here in symbols [and images].

Those who say [there is a heavenly person and] one that is higher are wrong,[56] for they call the visible heavenly person (68) "lower" and the one to whom the hidden realm belongs "higher." It would be better for them to speak of the inner, the outer, and the outermost.[57] For the master called corruption "the outermost darkness,"[58] and there is nothing outside it. He said, "My father who is in secret." He said, "Go into your room, shut the door behind you, and pray to your father who is in secret"[59]—that is, the one who is innermost. What is innermost is the fullness, and there is nothing further within. And this is what they call uppermost.

FALL AND RETURN TO FULLNESS

Before Christ some came from a realm they could not re-enter, and they went to a place they could not yet leave. Then Christ came. Those who went in he brought out, and those who went out he brought in.[60]

WHEN EVE WAS IN ADAM

When Eve was in Adam, there was no death. When she was separated from him, death came. If <she> enters into him again and he embraces <her>, death will cease to be.[61]

"WHY HAVE YOU FORSAKEN ME?"

"My God, my God, why, lord, have you forsaken me?"[62] He spoke these words on the cross, for he had left that place.

TRUE FLESH

[The master] was conceived from what [is imperishable], through God. The [master rose] from the dead, but [he did not come into being as he] was. Rather, his [body] was [completely] perfect. [It was] of flesh, and this [flesh] was true flesh. [Our flesh] is not true flesh but only an image of the true. (69)

THE WEDDING CHAMBER

Animals do not have a wedding chamber,[63] nor do slaves or defiled women. The wedding chamber is for free men and virgins.

❋ ❋

PURE MARRIAGE

No [one can] know when [a husband] (82) and wife have sex except those two, for marriage in this world is a mystery for those married. If defiled marriage is hidden, how much more is undefiled marriage a true mystery! It is not fleshly but pure. It belongs not to desire but to will. It belongs not to darkness or night but to the day and the light.

If marriage is exposed, it has become prostitution, and the bride plays the harlot not only if she is impregnated by another man but even if she slips out of her bedchamber and is seen. Let her show herself only to her father and her mother, the friend of the bridegroom, and the attendants of the bridegroom. They are allowed to enter the bridal chamber every day. But let the others yearn just to hear her voice and enjoy the fragrance of her ointment, and let them feed on the crumbs that fall from the table, like dogs.[64]

Bridegrooms and brides belong to the bridal chamber. No one can see a bridegroom or a bride except by becoming one.

❧ ❦

Eternal Light

Everyone who [enters] the bedchamber will kindle the [light. This is] like marriages that occur [in secret and] take place at night. The light of the fire [shines] (86) during the night and then goes out. The mysteries of that marriage, however, are performed in the day and the light, and neither that day nor its light ever sets.

If someone becomes an attendant of the bridal chamber, that person will receive the light. If one does not receive it while here in this place, one cannot receive it in the other place.

Those who receive the light cannot be seen or grasped. Nothing can trouble such people even while they are living in this world. And when they leave this world, they have already received truth through images, and the world has become the eternal realm. To these people the eternal realm is fullness.

This is the way it is. It is revealed to such a person alone, hidden not in darkness and night but hidden in perfect day and holy light.

❋CHAPTER 5❋

The Dialogue of the Savior

THE DIALOGUE OF THE SAVIOR is a rather fragmentary Nag Hammadi text, from codex 3 (tractate 5), in which Jesus discusses gnostic issues with his disciples. While sometimes the disciples are referred to in a general, anonymous fashion, more often three disciples are specified and called by their names: Judas, most likely Judas Thomas of Gospel of Thomas fame; Matthew; and Mary, almost certainly Mary Magdalene. Among figures with names like Matthew, Matthew (Matthaios) is a well-known disciple of Jesus, Matthias is the replacement for Judas Iscariot according to the Acts of the Apostles, and Mathaias is the recorder of sayings of Jesus in the Book of Thomas. Mary in the Dialogue of the Savior resembles portrayals of Mary Magdalene in other sources. The Dialogue of the Savior itself seems related to other gnostic texts and themes, and it shows particular similarities to the Gospel of Thomas. The date and place of the composition of the Dialogue of the Savior are unknown, but Helmut Koester and Elaine Pagels suggest that the Dialogue of the Savior may have been written in the first decades of the second century, on the basis of other materials that derive from the end of the first century.

The portion of the Dialogue of the Savior presented here is from the second half of the text, almost to the conclusion (which is very fragmentary and is not translated here). In this section Judas, Matthew, and Mary experience an apocalyptic vision with gnostic motifs. The light of God comes down from the realm of fullness above to the world of deficiency below, and that world must be saved through the word and restored to the light above. The vision and explanation of the vision prove convincing to the disciples, and Mary and the others discuss with the master Jesus the vision and other points of interest: the rulers or archons of the world, the garments worn by the soul, fullness and deficiency, life and death. In the midst of the conversation, Mary utters several aphoristic sayings ("The wickedness of the day <is sufficient>. Workers deserve their food. Disciples resemble their teachers."), sayings that are attributed to Jesus as his wisdom sayings in other sources. The text observes that Mary spoke this "as a woman who understood everything [or "who understood completely"]."

Near the conclusion of the Dialogue of the Savior the master says, "Pray in the place where there is no woman," and this provocative statement stimulates comments about the works of the female and the end of childbirth. This discussion recalls a statement earlier in the text, "Whatever is from woman dies," and it is also reminiscent of the Gospel of Thomas 114 and sayings in the Gospel of the Egyptians. In the Gospel of the Egyptians (in Clement of Alexandria, *Miscellanies* 3.6.45) Salome asks, "How long will death prevail?" and Jesus answers, "As long as you women bear children," and again in the Gospel of the Egyptians (in Clement of Alexandria, *Miscellanies* 3.9.63) Jesus states, "I have come to do away with the works of the female." Immediately Clement adds that by "female" Jesus means lust and by "works" birth and death, so that the destruction of the works of the female actually entails liberation from the cycle of mortality, the cycle of birth, decay, and death, in order to enjoy the light and life of the divine.

FOR FURTHER READING: Helmut Koester and Elaine Pagels, Introduction to the Dialogue of the Savior; Beate Blatz and Einar Thomassen, "The Dialogue of the Savior"; Silke Petersen and Hans-Gebhard Bethge, "Der Dialog des Erlösers."

The Dialogue of the Savior[1]

He [took] Judas, Matthew, and Mary[2] (135) [to show them the final] consummation of heaven and earth, and when he placed his [hand] on them, they hoped they might [see] it. Judas gazed up and saw a region of great height, and he saw the region of the abyss below.

Judas said to Matthew, "Brother, who can ascend to such a height or descend to the abyss below? For there is great fire there, and great terror."

At that moment a word[3] issued from the height. As Judas was standing there, he saw how the word came [down].

He asked the word, "Why have you come down?"

The child of humanity[4] greeted them and said to them, "A seed from a power was deficient, and it descended to the earth's abyss. The majesty remembered [it], and sent the [word to] it. The word brought the seed up into [the presence] of the majesty, so that (136) the first word might not be lost."[5]

[His] disciples marveled at everything he told them, and they accepted all of it in faith. And they understood that there is no need to keep wickedness before one's eyes.

Then he said to his disciples, "Did I not tell you that, like a visible flash of thunder and lightning, what is good will be taken up to the light?"

All his disciples praised him and said, "Master, before you appeared here, who was there to praise you, for all praises are because of you? Or who was there to bless [you], for all blessing comes from you?"

As they were standing there, he saw two spirits bringing a single soul with them, and there was a great flash of lightning. A word came from the child of humanity, saying, "Give them their garments," and the small became like the great. They were [like] those who were received up; (137) [there was no distinction] among them.[6]

These [words convinced the] disciples to whom he [spoke].

MARY ASKS ABOUT THE VISION

Mary [said to him, "Look, I] see the evil [that affects] people from the start, when they dwell with each other."

The master said [to her], "When you see them, [you understand] a great deal; they will [not stay there]. But when you see the one who exists eternally, that is the great vision."

They all said to him, "Explain it to us."

He said to them, "How do you wish to see it, [in] a passing vision or in an eternal vision?"

He went on to say, "Do your best to save what can come after [me], and seek it and speak through it, so that whatever you seek may be in harmony with you. For I [say] to you, truly the living God [is] in you, (138) [as you also are] in God."[7]

JUDAS ASKS ABOUT THE RULERS OF THE WORLD, AND THE GARMENTS

Judas [said], "I really want [to learn everything]."

The [master] said to him, "The living [God does not] dwell [in this] entire [region] of deficiency."[8]

Judas [asked], "Who [will rule over us]?"

The master replied, "[Look, here are] all the things that exist [among] what remains. You [rule] over them."

Judas said, "But look, the rulers are over us, so they will rule over us."

The master answered, "You will rule over them. When you remove jealousy from yourselves, you will clothe yourselves in light and enter the bridal chamber."[9]

Judas asked, "How will [our] garments be brought to us?"

The master answered, "There are some who will provide them for you and others who will receive [them], (139) and they [will give] you your garments. For who can reach that place? It is very [frightening]. But the garments of life were given to these people because they know the way they will go.[10] Indeed, it is even difficult for me to reach it."[11]

MARY UTTERS WORDS OF WISDOM

Mary said, "So,

The wickedness of each day <is sufficient>.[12]
Workers deserve their food.[13]
Disciples resemble their teachers."[14]

She spoke this utterance as a woman who understood everything.[15]

THE DISCIPLES ASK ABOUT FULLNESS
AND DEFICIENCY, LIFE AND DEATH

The disciples asked him, "What is fullness and what is deficiency?"

He answered them, "You are from fullness and you are in a place of deficiency.[16] And look, his light has poured down on me."

Matthew asked, "Tell me, master, how the dead die and how the living live." (140)

The master said, "[You have] asked me about a [true] saying that eye has not seen, nor have I heard it, except from you.[17] But I say to you, when what moves a person slips away, that person will be called dead, and when what is living leaves what is dead, it will be called alive."

Judas asked, "So why, really, do some <die> and some live?"

The master said, "Whatever is from truth does not die. Whatever is from woman dies."[18]

Mary asked, "Tell me, master, why have I come to this place, to gain or to lose?"[19]

The master replied, "You show the greatness of the revealer."

Mary asked him, "Master, then is there a place that is abandoned or without truth?"

The master said, "The place where I am not."

Mary said, "Master, you are awesome and marvelous, (141) and [like a devouring fire] to those who do not know [you]."

Matthew asked, "Why do we not go to our rest at once?"[20]

The master said, "When you leave these burdens behind."

Matthew asked, "How does the small unite with the great?"

The master said, "When you leave behind what cannot accompany you, then you will rest."[21]

MARY AND THE OTHER DISCIPLES
DISCUSS TRUE LIFE WITH THE MASTER

Mary said, "I want to understand all things, [just as] they are."

The master said, "Whoever seeks life, this is their wealth. For the world's [rest] is false, and its gold and silver are deceptive."[22]

His disciples asked him, "What should we do for our work to be perfect?"

The master [said] to them, "Be ready, in every circumstance. Blessings on those who have found (142) the [strife and have seen] the struggle with their eyes. They have not killed nor have [they] been killed, but they have emerged victorious."

Judas asked, "Tell me, master, what is the beginning of the way?"[23]

He said, "Love and goodness. If one of these had existed among the rulers, wickedness would never have come to be."

Matthew said, "Master, you have spoken of the end of the universe with no difficulty."

The master said, "You have understood all the things I said to you and you have accepted them in faith. If you know them, they are yours. If not, they are not yours."

They asked him, "To what place are we going?"

The master said, "Stand in the place you can reach."

Mary asked, "Is everything established in this way visible?"

The master said, "I have told you, the one who can see reveals."

His twelve disciples asked him, "Teacher, [with] (143) serenity . . . teach us. . . ."

The master said, "[If you have understood] everything I have [told you], you will [become immortal, for] you . . . everything."

Mary said, "There is only one saying I shall [speak] to the master, about the mystery of truth. In this we stand and in this we appear to those who are worldly."

Judas said to Matthew, "We want to understand what sort of garments we are to be clothed with when we leave the corruption of the flesh."

The master said, "The rulers and the administrators[24] have garments that are given only for a while and do not last. But you, as children of truth, are not to clothe yourselves with these garments that last only for a while. Rather, I say to you, you will be blessed when you strip off your clothing. For it is no great thing (144) [to lay aside what is] external."[25]

. . ."[26] said, "Do I speak and do I receive . . . ?"

The master said, "Yes, [one who receives] your father in [a reflective way]."[27]

MARY QUESTIONS THE MASTER
ABOUT THE MUSTARD SEED

Mary asked, "[Of what] kind is the mustard seed?[28] Is it from heaven or from earth?"

The master said, "When the father established the world for himself, he left many things with the mother of all. That is why he sows and works."[29]

Judas said, "You have told us this from the mind of truth. When we pray, how should we pray?"

The master said, "Pray in the place where there is no woman."

Matthew says, "He tells us, 'Pray in the place where there is no woman,' which means, destroy the works of the female,[30] not because there is another form of birth[31] but because they should stop [giving birth]."

Mary said, "Will they never be destroyed?"

The master said, "[You] know they will perish [once again], (145) and [the works] of [the female here] will be [destroyed as well]."[32]

Judas said [to Matthew], "The works of the [female] will perish. [Then] the rulers will [call upon their realms], and we shall be ready for them."

The master said, "Will they see [you and will they] see those who receive you? Look, a true word[33] is coming from the father to the abyss, silently, with a flash of lightning, and it is productive.[34] Do they see it or overcome it? No, you know more fully [the way] that [neither angel] nor authority [knows]. It is the way of the father and the son, for the two are one. And you will travel the [way] you have come to know. Even if the rulers become great, they will not be able to reach it. I tell you the [truth], it is even difficult for me to reach it."[35] (146)

[Mary] asked [the master], "If the works [are destroyed, what actually] destroys a work?"

[The master said], "You know. [On the day] I destroy [it, people] will go to their own places."

Judas said, "How is the spirit disclosed?"

The master said, "How [is] the sword [disclosed]?"

Judas said, "How is the light disclosed?"

The master said, "[It is disclosed] through itself eternally."

Judas asked, "Who forgives whose works? Do the works [forgive] the world or does the world forgive the works?"

The master [answered], "Who is [it]? Really, whoever has come to know the works. For it is the responsibility of these people to do the [will] of the father."

❋CHAPTER 6❋

Pistis Sophia

PISTIS SOPHIA CONSISTS OF A LONG, sprawling, and fairly tedious series of gnostic reflections and revelations about Pistis Sophia, "Faith Wisdom," a female manifestation of the divine who sometimes is said to have fallen from the realm of the divine, to have repented of her mistake, and to be destined for salvation and deliverance. The text Pistis Sophia fills the Askew Codex (Codex Askewianus), a manuscript from the second half of the fourth century. The text itself may, at least in part, be a century older, and it was probably composed in Egypt.

The figure of Pistis Sophia is mentioned in other gnostic works besides the present text—for example, in the Reality of the Rulers, On the Origin of the World, Eugnostos, and (less directly) the Sophia of Jesus Christ, all texts from the Nag Hammadi library. In the text On the Origin of the World, Pistis Sophia is featured as a divine power of light from whose deficiency come chaos and the creator of this world, and whose reflection in the water becomes the pattern for the creation of the human being in the image of God. In Eugnostos and the Sophia of Jesus Christ, the child of humanity, or the savior, becomes one with Sophia, his consort, whom some call Pistis, and the child of humanity emits a bright, androgynous light. Here in Pistis Sophia, the fall of Sophia, her repentance, and further aspects of her story are reiterated, and they are understood to be echoed in texts like the Psalms.

A number of followers of Jesus raise questions and make observations in Pistis Sophia, but a special place is reserved for Mary Magdalene and John the Virgin, and of these two, Mary Magdalene is most prominent. It is said of Mary and John that they are the greatest of the followers, yet Mary, described as beautiful of speech, is acclaimed by Jesus as being more devoted to heaven's kingdom than all her brothers. According to Carl Schmidt and other scholars who have done the counting, Mary Magdalene is credited in Pistis Sophia with raising no fewer than thirty-nine of the forty-six questions addressed to Jesus.

In the selections from Pistis Sophia translated here, Mary Magdalene teaches about the nature of life in the world and the salvation of the human race by citing and interpreting passages in Isaiah as well as two sayings of Jesus: "Whoever has ears to hear should hear" and "The first will be last and the last will be first." These sayings are known throughout early Christian literature—for example, in the New Testament Gospels and the Gospel of Thomas. As elsewhere—in Pistis Sophia (146), and in the Gospel of Thomas and the Gospel of Mary—here, in Pistis Sophia 36, Peter complains about Mary and her loquaciousness, but Jesus praises her. Mary Magdalene, Jesus states, is most committed to heaven's kingdom, most blessed of women on earth, and a pure spiritual woman.

FOR FURTHER READING: Deirdre Good, "Pistis Sophia"; Henri-Charles Puech and Beate Blatz, "Pistis Sophia"; Kurt Rudolph, *Gnosis;* Carl Schmidt and Violet MacDermot, eds., *Pistis Sophia.*

Pistis Sophia[1]

MARY IS EXALTED ABOVE HER BROTHERS

When Jesus had said these things to his disciples, he told them, "Whoever has ears to hear should hear."

Now it happened, when Mary[2] heard these words as the savior was speaking, she gazed into the air for an hour and said, "My master, command me to speak openly."

The compassionate Jesus answered and said to Mary, "Blessed Mary, you whom I shall complete with all the mysteries on high, speak openly, for you are one whose heart is set on heaven's kingdom more than all your brothers."[3] (18)

MARY EXPLAINS LIBERATION FROM FATE

Then Mary said to the savior, "My master, when you said to us, 'Whoever has ears to hear should hear,' you said this so that we might understand what you have spoken. So listen, my master, and I shall speak openly. This is what you said: 'I have taken a third of the power of the rulers of all the realms, and I have turned their fate and the sphere they rule, so that when members of the human race invoke them in their mysteries, which the disobedient angels taught them to complete their evil and lawless deeds with the mystery of their magic, they may not be able to complete their lawless deeds from now on.' You have taken their power from them and from their astrologers and fortune-tellers and soothsayers, and from now on they will not understand or explain anything that happens. For you have turned their sphere, and you have made them spend six months oriented to the left to exert their influence, and six months oriented to the right to exert their influence.[4]

"My master, the power within the prophet Isaiah has spoken concerning this saying and has explained it once in a spiritual parable, speaking about the vision of Egypt: Where, Egypt, where are your fortune-tellers and astrologers and moaners and groaners?[5] Let them tell you now what the Lord Sabaoth will do.[6]

"Before you came, the power within the prophet Isaiah prophesied about you, that you would take away the power of the rulers of the realms and turn their sphere and their fate, so that from now on they would know nothing. Concerning this it has also been said, You will not know what the Lord Sabaoth will do.[7] That is to say, none of the rulers will know what you will do from now on. The rulers signify Egypt, for they are matter. The power within Isaiah once prophesied about you and said, You will not know from now on what the Lord Sabaoth will do.[8] Concerning the power of light that you have taken from good Sabaoth, who is on the right, and that today is in your material body, concerning this, my master Jesus, you have said to us, 'Whoever has ears to hear should hear,' so that you may know whose heart is directed toward heaven's kingdom."[9]

(19)

When Mary finished saying these things, Jesus said, "Well done, Mary. You are more blessed than all women on earth, because you will be the fullness of fullnesses and the completion of completions."[10]

❋ ❋

PETER COMPLAINS ABOUT MARY'S PROMINENCE

(36) When Jesus finished saying these things to his disciples, he asked, "Do you understand how I am speaking with you?"

Peter stepped forward and said to Jesus, "My master, we cannot endure this woman who gets in our way and does not let any of us speak, though she talks all the time."[11]

Jesus answered and said to his disciples, "Let anyone in whom the power of the spirit has arisen, so that the person understands what I say, come forward and speak. Peter, I perceive that your power within you understands the interpretation of the mystery of repentance that Pistis Sophia mentioned. So now, Peter, discuss among your brothers the thought of her repentance."[12]

✳ ✳

MARY FEARS PETER BUT IS VINDICATED

(72) When the first mystery finished saying these things to the disciples, Mary came forward and said, "My master, I understand in my mind that I can come forward at any time to interpret what Pistis Sophia has said, but I am afraid of Peter, because he threatens me and hates our gender."

When she said this, the first mystery replied to her, "Any of those filled with the spirit of light will come forward to interpret what I say: no one will be able to oppose them."

✳ ✳

MARY MAGDALENE IS A PURE SPIRITUAL WOMAN

(87) When Jesus finished saying these things, Mary Magdalene stepped forward and said, "My master, my enlightened person[13] has ears, and I accept all the words you speak. Now, my master, this is what you said: 'All souls of the human race who will receive the mysteries of the light will be first in the inheritance of the light, before all the rulers who have repented, before the entire place on the right, before the entire place of the treasury of light.' Concerning this saying, my master, you

once said to us, 'The first will be last and the last will be first.'[14] That is to say, the last is the whole human race that will be first within the kingdom of light, before the inhabitants of the places on high, which are first. For this reason, my master, you have said to us, 'Whoever has ears to hear should hear.' In other words, you wanted to know whether we have grasped all the sayings you spoke. My master, this is the word."

When Mary finished saying these things, the savior marveled greatly at the answers she gave, for she had become entirely pure spirit. Jesus answered and said to her, "Well done, Mary, pure spiritual woman.[15] This is the interpretation of the word."

CHAPTER 7

The Manichaean Psalms of Heracleides

THE PSALMS OF HERACLEIDES are part of the beautiful collection of songs in the Manichaean Psalmbook, a songbook used in worship by followers of Manichaeism. Manichaeism was a world religion that was founded by Mani, a third-century prophet who grew up in the context of a Jewish-Christian baptismal community, received a revelation from an angel he referred to as the twin, and eventually was called the apostle of light for the Manichaean religion. Extending from Europe and North Africa to Central Asia and China, Manichaeism developed as a universal religion that incorporated Christian, Zoroastrian, and Buddhist ideas. In a number of ways Manichaeism resembles gnosticism.

In the Psalms of Heracleides, Mary Magdalene is mentioned several times. In one portion of these psalms, various characteristic features of disciples and apostles of Jesus are enumerated, and a description of Mary is included. It is said (192.21–22) that "Mary is one who casts a net in an effort to catch the other eleven who were lost." Martha, Salome, and Arsinoe are also mentioned, and Martha is called Mary's sister. These four women disciples may also be named in the First Apocalypse of James from the Nag Hammadi library. Again in the Psalms of Heracleides, in a similar list of disciples (194.19), Mary is proclaimed to be "the spirit of wisdom [or 'Sophia']."

In the song from the Psalms of Heracleides translated here (187), the tender discussion between a man (Jesus) and a woman (Mary) is based on the story of Mary Magdalene meeting the risen Christ in the garden, in John 20:1–18. In the song Mary is mandated to be the messenger to the lost orphans, the eleven male disciples, and to use her skill and knowledge to gather the lost sheep to the shepherd. She is capable of speaking with authority to Simon Peter and the others. And she is to be given glory, according to the song,

> because she has listened to her master,
> [she has] carried out his instructions
> with joy in her whole heart.

FOR FURTHER READING: C. R. C. Allberry, ed., *A Manichaean Psalm-Book: Part II;* Willis Barnstone and Marvin Meyer, *The Gnostic Bible;* Jason BeDuhn, *The Manichaean Body;* Hans-Joachim Klimkeit, *Gnosis on the Silk Road.*

A Song from the Manichaean
Psalms of Heracleides[1]

Mary, Mary, know me,
but do not touch [me].[2]
[Dry] the tears of your eyes,
and know that I am your master,
only do not touch me,
for I have not yet seen my father's face.

Your God was not taken away,
as you thought in your pettiness.[3]
Your God did not die;
rather, he mastered [death].
I am not the gardener.
I have given, I have received . . . ,
I did [not] appear to you
until I saw your tears and grief . . . for me.

Cast this sadness away
and perform this service.
Be my messenger to these lost orphans.
Hurry, with joy, go to the eleven.
You will find them gathered on the bank of the Jordan.
The traitor convinced them to fish
as they did earlier,
and to lay down the nets
in which they caught people for life.

Say to them, "Arise, let us go.
Your brother calls you."
If they disregard me as brother,
say to them, "It is your master."
If they disregard me as master,
say to them, "It is your lord."
Use all your skill and knowledge
until you bring the sheep to the shepherd.

If you see that they do not respond,
make Simon Peter come to you.
Say to him, "Remember my words,
between me and you. Remember what I said,
between me and you, on the Mount of Olives.
I have something to say,
I have no one to whom to say it."[4]

Rabbi, my master, I shall carry out your instructions
with joy in my whole heart.
I shall not let my heart rest,
I shall not let my eyes sleep,
I shall not let my feet relax
until I bring the sheep to the fold.

Glory to Mary,
because she has listened to her master,
[she has] carried out his instructions
with joy in her whole heart.

[Glory and] triumph to the soul of blessed Mary.

CHAPTER 8

"Should We All Turn and Listen to Her?"
Mary Magdalene in the Spotlight

ESTHER A. DE BOER

READING ALL THE SOURCE TEXTS on Mary Magdalene is quite an experience, and one cannot help but feel a sense of loss, betrayal, anger, and sadness. But at the same time questions arise. What do we think of these texts? What do we think of these different portrayals of Mary Magdalene?

During the past few decades the interest in Mary Magdalene seems to have been growing constantly, and the discovery of the second-century Gospel of Mary in particular has made quite an impact. Until then only Gospels named after men were known: Matthew, Mark, Luke, John, Peter, Thomas, James, Philip, Judas. It seemed that there had been little room for women in church history. And suddenly there she was: Mary Magdalene, together with her Gospel.

Above all it was Elaine Pagels's book, *The Gnostic Gospels,* that allowed the larger public to get to know Mary Magdalene in this new way. Pagels's chapter on feminine symbolism for God and feminine leadership in gnostic circles made all the difference. Gnosticism was presented as a movement in which women had plenty of room, and the position of Mary Magdalene offered an important clue. As a result, women and men became suspicious of orthodox Christianity with its exclusively male symbolism for God, and its male leadership, rules and rituals, and dogmas.

Books about Mary Magdalene have become popular. Marianne Fredriksson's novel, *According to Mary Magdalene,* for example, became a best-seller. This novel tells the story of how Mary Magdalene comes to realize that Peter and Paul are altering Christ's teaching to suit their own goals and how she struggles to spread his undistorted teaching herself. In the introduction to the novel, Fredriksson explains that she decided to write this book after reading the Gospel of Mary.

FEMALE IMAGERY, FEMALE LEADERSHIP?

In 1985 the conference "Images of the Feminine in Gnosticism," held in Claremont, California, initiated a series of scholarly studies.[1] The numerous female characters and images in the gnostic texts of Nag Hammadi are impressive. The soul is important as a female character, Norea as a savior, and Sophia as a goddess. The conference, however, showed that feminine images in gnostic texts do not stand alone. They are related to male images, and together they form the two necessary parts of the heterosexual symbolism that is so characteristic of gnostic thought. Could this heterosexual symbolism leave room for women to be autonomous individuals? The lectures given at the conference showed that the answer to this question depends in large part on who is interpreting the female imagery.

For instance, the Norea of Anne McGuire is a strong and self-conscious fighter against the archons, while the Norea of Birger Pearson is a dull consort of Seth. The figure of Sophia in Richard Smith's lecture is the goddess whose fall is her own fault: she thought she could manage without her male consort. Yet in the lecture of Pheme Perkins, the fallen Sophia is the means by which human beings can identify with God. In Maddalena Scopello's lecture, the figure of the soul in Exegesis on the Soul is depicted as an independent and self-conscious woman who lives and saves her own life. Yet Richard Smith depicts the soul in the same text as a woman who is happy only at the side of the husband her father chose for her.

Thus, the conference made clear that gnostic female imagery may be interpreted in very different ways. At the very least one must admit that gnostic female imagery in its heterosexual setting is quite open to androcentric hermeneutics.

Anne McGuire warns against unifying the gnostic texts under a single category such as gender. In her opinion gender imagery "was used to represent a variety of more abstract issues in religious speculation, including the relation of duality or multiplicity to unity and of the many to the one."[2] The texts say little about actual men and women.

The fact that so many women disciples have a role in Christian gnostic literature might lead one to conclude that they were quite important in Christian gnostic circles. However, according to Silke Petersen, who has studied the role and position of women disciples in gnostic writings, one should first compare this circumstance with the presence of male disciples in gnostic writings and the references to women disciples in non-gnostic texts. She concludes that for every gnostic writing in which a woman has an important role, there are two others in which a man assumes such a position. At the same time, whereas in all the New Testament Gospels women play a role in the Easter story, there are several similar stories in gnostic writings in which women play no role at all.[3]

Furthermore, when reading certain church fathers, one might think that early Christianity valued exclusively male leadership. However, Bernadette Brooten and Karen Jo Torjesen argue on the basis of inscriptions that there must have been female leadership in the early church until the fourth century. In a major study of early church women, Anne Jensen brings to light actual women who were missionaries, prophets, martyrs, deacons, theologians, teachers, and writers. Whereas Jensen studies contemporary writings, Ute Eisen researches inscriptions and documentary papyri, and she concludes that women were apostles, prophets and teachers of theology, consecrated widows, deacons, stewards, priests, and bishops. Both argue on the basis of inscriptions and texts that female leadership continued until the tenth century.

MARY MAGDALENE IN GNOSTIC WRITINGS

Even if early Christianity is not the dark background to the light that Mary Magdalene sheds, examining the early texts about her remains very exciting. The church may have held her to be a sinner and a penitent,[4] yet according to gnostic texts she is the disciple of Jesus gifted with great insight. Anyone weary of misogynist texts of church fathers will feel refreshed by reading gnostic texts featuring Mary Magdalene.

In Pistis Sophia and the Gospel of Mary, Mary Magdalene has an important role. In Pistis Sophia, thirty-nine of the forty-six questions are asked by her. In the Gospel of Mary, at least half of what remains of the Gospel is a revelation dialogue between Mary and the master Jesus, while in the other half she is one of the central figures. The discovery of the Gospel of Mary makes Mary Magdalene the only historical woman who has a Gospel written in her name.[5]

In these writings Mary Magdalene is one of the disciples, learning from Jesus. She is asking questions, she is spoken to and spoken of. Both in the Gospel of Thomas 21 and in the Wisdom of Jesus Christ 114 she asks about the nature and purpose of discipleship. In the Wisdom of Jesus Christ 98 she asks how the disciples can find knowledge. In the Dialogue of the Savior she is one of the three disciples (the other two are Matthew and Judas) who receive special instruction. She asks about the meaning of sorrow and joy (126), and she also asks her brothers where and how they will observe all the things that the master tells them (131).

Furthermore, Mary Magdalene has a role as interpreter. She knows the scripture and the sayings of Jesus, and she discusses their meaning. In Pistis Sophia she quotes Isaiah and the Psalms, and she memorizes what Jesus has said and Paul has written (17; 18; 60; 62; 113). She also quotes sayings of Jesus in the Dialogue of the Savior 139. The author adds that she said this "as a woman who understood everything." Mary Magdalene's insight is highly esteemed, and in Pistis Sophia she is repeatedly praised by the master. She puts the right questions accurately and purposefully (25), and her heart is said to be more attuned to heaven's kingdom than her brothers (17). In the Gospel of Philip 64 and the Gospel of Mary 18 the disciples state that the master loves her more than any of them. In the Gospel of Philip 59 she is said to be the constant companion of the master Jesus. The First Apocalypse of James 38 and 42 relates that the master had twelve male and seven female disciples. When James says of the female disciples, "I am amazed how powerless vessels have become strong by a perception that is in them," the master instructs him to learn from them, and mentions a few names, among them Mary Magdalene's (38; 40). In both Pistis Sophia and the Gospel of Mary, Mary Magdalene shares her insight and teaches the disciples. For this she is praised, but also attacked, and in some writings it is Peter who shows hostility.

The text I love most is in Pistis Sophia. Mary Magdalene says, "My master, I understand in my mind that I can come forward at any time to interpret what Pistis Sophia has said, but I am afraid of Peter, because he threatens me and hates our gender." When she said this, the first mystery replied to her, "Any of those filled with the spirit of light will come forward to interpret what I say: no one will be able to oppose them." This is very different from what the church father Origen envisaged in the same century. In commenting on Paul's First Letter to the Corinthians, he says, "'For it is shameful for a woman to speak in the community' (14:35). Whatever she says, even if she says admirable or holy things—it comes out of the mouth of a woman" (Catena of Fragments on 1 Corinthians, 74.34–37).[6]

Mary Magdalene's position in gnostic texts is impressive. Yet, one should not overlook the fact that her position is by no means unchallenged. In most of the texts Mary Magdalene has to be defended for her right to speak up, and the readers have to be persuaded that Mary Magdalene is a person to be listened to, in spite of the fact that she is a woman (Gospel of Thomas 114; Gospel of Mary 17–18; Gospel of Philip 63–64; Pistis Sophia 36; 72). Some would say that this reinforces the assumption that orthodox early Christianity is misogynist and gnostic early Christianity is not, and they would argue that Peter's hostility toward Mary in gnostic texts is to be interpreted symbolically. In this quite common view, Peter stands for the orthodoxy of the church and Mary Magdalene for gnosticism.[7]

The Gospel of Mary suggests a different interpretation of Peter's hostility towards Mary. It is his hot temper that makes him object to Mary.[8] Indeed, he represents an orthodox view, not with respect to a doctrine of faith but rather with respect to the liability of women.[9]

Peter's objection to Mary as a person who could have something important to say about the teachings of Jesus represents a common view of the culture at the time. Women were simply regarded as second-rate creatures.[10] In his book about Mary Magdalene in gnostic texts, Antti Marjanen draws attention to the fact that many of the gnostic writings that give Mary Magdalene a prominent role make use of language that devalues women.[11] He argues that the positive gnostic view of Mary Magdalene did not change the attitudes towards women in general. Silke Petersen, in her study about Jesus' women disciples in gnostic texts, even concludes that Mary Magdalene is such a prominent disciple precisely because she has transcended her inferior femaleness.[12]

DUALISM

No one reading the Nag Hammadi Library will be surprised by such a conclusion. One will remember texts like these: "Flee the bondage of femininity, and choose for yourselves the salvation of masculinity" (Zostrianos 131). Or: "Destroy the works of womanhood" (Dialogue of the Savior 144). This is apparently meant not only symbolically, as is shown by the text preceding this command: "Pray in the place where there is no woman." There are more texts. The Gospel of Philip says, "Christ came to restore the separation, which had been there from the beginning, and to reunite the two, and to give life to those who died as a result of the separation and to unite them" (70). And the

Gospel of Thomas says, "When you make the two into one . . . , and when you make male and female into a single one, so that the male will not be male nor the female be female . . . , then you will enter [the kingdom]" (22). These texts are often quoted as if they show that women and men are equal in gnosticism or that gnosticism strives for oneness and opposes dualism. And indeed, these texts are wonderful witnesses when one reads them with modern eyes. However, it is also important to look for the particular meaning of this oneness of male and female in antiquity.

Philo of Alexandria is a representative example of the thoughts in antiquity about the meaning and function of the terms "male" and "female." He uses the terms in a metaphorical sense, but at the same time they also relate to real men and women. The man symbolizes reason and the woman perception through the senses. In Questions and Answers on Genesis, Philo proposes that men are "manly" by disposition, which means that they are wise, sound, just, prudent, pious, filled with freedom and boldness, and akin to wisdom, but women are "womanly," which means that they are irrational and consumed by bestial passions, fear, sorrow, pleasure, and desire.

However, Philo suggests that women can become "manly" and men can degenerate into womanliness (Questions and Answers on Genesis 2.49; 4.148). There can be times when the "manly" must avoid the "womanly" in order not to be allured by it. But in the end the "manly" and the "womanly" should be one. Philo says about this process of uniting, "not that the masculine thoughts may be made womanish and relaxed by softness, but that the female element, the senses, may be made manly by following masculine thoughts and by receiving from them seed for procreation, that it may perceive (things) with wisdom, prudence, justice, and courage, in sum, with virtue" (Questions and

Answers on Genesis 2.49). This uniting of male and female is not based on equality or equivalence.[13] In the world of antiquity it was better to be male than to be female, and the male had to take the lead to improve the female. Uniting the two does not end up in androgyny in our modern sense of the word. It does not presuppose a holistic view of male and female, but it presupposes a profoundly dualistic view, with the ideal being the female subsumed into the male, the womanly into the manly.

VOICES OPPOSING MALE-FEMALE DUALISM

Dualism as such is not surprising in Hellenistic thought. In general, spirit was supposed to be nearer to God than matter, and man and manhood were considered to be nearer to God than woman and womanhood.[14] What is surprising, however, is that there are other voices to be heard, voices that challenge this dualistic way of thinking—for instance, the voices represented by the text of Pistis Sophia as quoted earlier, voices that defend openness to women. It is important to note that both orthodox and gnostic traditions are androcentric and contain misogynistic texts. Yet both traditions have also preserved texts that give voice to a positive view of women as persons to be fully reckoned with.[15]

Indeed, the early church has preserved such texts. For instance, the church father Jerome writes in his letter to a woman named Principia about the life of Marcella:

Those unbelievers who read me may perhaps smile to find me lingering over the praises of weak women. But if they will recall how holy women attended our lord and savior and ministered to him of their substance, and how the three Marys stood before the cross, and particularly how Mary of Magdala, called "of the tower" because of her earnestness and ardent faith, was privileged to see the rising Christ first even before the apostles, they will convict themselves of pride rather than me of folly, who judge of virtue not by the sex but by the mind. (Epistle 127)

Jerome's words are quite revolutionary, especially given his own apparent misogyny in other contexts, and given the dualistic view of male and female in antiquity.[16] In defending his view, he draws on texts that can be found in the Gospels of the New Testament. He refers to the canonical Gospels. This might seem strange. Are the canonical Gospels not the heart of orthodox early Christianity? Have they not been singled out, because they suited the early church? I do not think so. They are too unorthodox. In fact, the canonical Gospels preserve texts that firmly represent voices of protest against the dualistic view of male and female in antiquity.

The New Testament gospels have preserved narratives in which Jesus gives his opinion on purity laws, marriage, and family ties. These are exactly the three customs that defined women's lives so very differently from the lives of men. Yet Jesus spiritualizes the laws of purity. Physical purity does not matter, but rather purity of heart (Mark 7:21–23; cf. Matt. 15:18–20). He declares marriage to be a bond of faithfulness between two people who both are responsible and who both can take initiatives (Mark 10:11–12). He extends family ties from blood relations to the religious community as a whole (Mark 3:34–35; cf. Matt. 12:49–50; Luke 8:21).

The New Testament Gospels also preserve texts in which Jesus liberates individual women from their female fate—

narratives like the one about Martha and Mary (Luke 10:38–42) or an adulteress (John 8:1–11). Moreover, the New Testament Gospels preserve narratives in which Jesus teaches women as he teaches men, such as the narrative about the Samaritan woman (John 4:1–30). It is evident that Jesus' teaching was meant not only for men but also for women; this is shown by the fact that in his illustrations and stories he seeks to refer to the experience of both. He speaks just as easily of the pains of giving birth, of leaven, salt, light, water, and keeping the house clean, as he does of stewardship, keeping sheep, fishing, and being a farmer. Although the New Testament Gospels are obviously androcentric, they provide evidence for the position that there were Christians who believed that Jesus made no distinction between men and women. The stories that represent this attitude have apparently been told and retold.

EARLY CHRISTIANITIES

However, when dealing with gnostic texts, most scholars would point to the specific dualism that is at the center of gnostic thought. Whereas, according to orthodox Christianity, the world is created by the father of Jesus and is originally good, according to gnostic Christian thought a lower deity has created the world and the creation is a fall. Woman and womanhood identified with sexuality and procreation must be utterly rejected in a view that regards the existence of the world as a mistake. Moreover, the later church deemed the belief that the creator God of Genesis would be considered a lower deity as clear heresy and a denial of the Jewish roots of Christian teaching.

In his book *Rethinking "Gnosticism,"* Michael Williams challenges scholars to abolish the term "gnosticism" or at least to use the designation cautiously and critically. He states that in antiquity there was no such thing as a clearly defined gnostic religion and that the label "gnostic" allows modern scholars to categorize certain writings in late antiquity in order to understand them more easily. He warns against misunderstanding certain texts by assuming that they belong to a fixed "gnostic" religion rather than allowing the texts to speak for themselves.

In *What Is Gnosticism?* Karen King concludes that "gnosticism" is a blanket term that covers many early Christian movements. She argues that the term existed only as a tool of orthodox identity formation, deriving from early Christian discourse about orthodoxy and heresy that has now taken on an independent existence. Further, she shows that the early Christian polemicists' discourse about orthodoxy and heresy has been intertwined with twentieth-century scholarship on gnosticism. This is an important insight, since, as she writes, "At stake is not only the capacity to write a more accurate history of ancient Christianity in all its multiformity, but also our capacity to engage critically the ancient politics of religious difference rather than unwittingly reproduce its strategies and results."[17] When reading the early texts about Mary Magdalene, it is helpful to keep this in mind. No clear boundaries between orthodox and other Christianities were fixed. It is far too simple to conclude that orthodox Christianity would have given Mary Magdalene little credit while gnostic Christianity would have had high esteem for her.

MARY MAGDALENE ACCORDING TO THE GOSPEL OF MARY

As we have said, Mary Magdalene is the only woman that has a Gospel written in her name.[18] Or, more precisely: Mary

Magdalene is the only woman whose Gospel has survived the ages. This Gospel is mostly interpreted as a gnostic writing, but others are convinced it should be interpreted in a broader context, as one of many testimonies of early Christian faith.[19] I suggest that the dualism in the Gospel of Mary is a moderate one and belongs to a Jewish-Christian and not a gnostic Christian context. In the Gospel of Mary the natural world is originally rooted into the divine, but has become mixed with a power contrary to nature. Both nature and this power contrary to nature act upon (passive) matter, as the sower sows wheat and his enemy weeds in Jesus' parable of the wheat and the weeds (Matthew 13:24–30; Gospel of Thomas 57). Thus, according to the Gospel of Mary the disciples should not deny the body or avoid the world, but, instead, be careful not to become overpowered by this "something contrary to nature" that has brought confusion and passion in the body and the world and disturbed their original harmony and peace.

Because of the Gospel's title, it would not be surprising if the beginning of the Gospel of Mary originally also was about Mary Magdalene. The first pages of the Gospel of Mary could have been about Mary telling the disciples of Jesus' crucifixion, of his death, and of her visit to Jesus' tomb, in a way comparable to accounts in the New Testament Gospels. One could think of the Gospel of John in which Mary is said to have gone to the disciples to tell them that she had seen the master and he had spoken to her (John 20:18).

One could also think of the second-century Epistle of the Apostles (Epistula Apostolorum), which, after describing several stories from Jesus' life, turns to his death and portrays Mary telling the disciples about his resurrection. When they do not believe her, she returns to the master Jesus, who then sends Sarah. In the Coptic version, these women are Martha and Mary.

When the apostles still do not believe, the master accompanies the women, whom the author calls "Mary and her sisters" (11), and he rebukes the apostles. In this context a dialogue between the disciples and Jesus occurs, where various themes arise, such as Jesus' incarnation, his return, the end of the world, the future of the disciples, the place of laws, the instruction to proclaim the gospel, and the suffering of the disciples, who finally are to be raised up, with Jesus, to reach final rest.

In the Gospel of Mary the dialogue with the savior, which starts somewhere before the Gospel of Mary 7, may well have been situated in a similar situation as in the Epistle of the Apostles. The savior, on the missing pages at the beginning of the Gospel of Mary, may have appeared after Mary's testimony of the resurrection to affirm the reliability of her words and expand upon certain themes. The difference with the Epistle of the Apostles is that the Gospel of Mary does not end with the master's departure, as does the Epistle of the Apostles (51), but, after the savior's departure, continues the story and tells of the disciples' reaction to the savior's instructions and of Mary's teaching.

In the Gospel of Mary the development of the story after the savior's departure is quite dramatic. The story not only gives the content of Mary's teaching but also presents several different views of who she is. After her teaching on the greatness of the child of humanity (or son of man), she turns the disciples' hearts inward to the good one, which is the child of humanity within them. The son of man, the crucified and resurrected Jesus, being within his disciples, is a well-known theme both in John as in the Pauline letters (e.g. John 14:20; 17: 26; Galatians 2:20; 4:19; Romans 8, 10).

Thanks to Mary, the disciples begin to discuss the words of the savior, apparently with the aim of proclaiming the Gospel.

It seems that initially only the men are doing this, since Peter asks Mary to join them, because in his view she is special among the women. According to Peter, the savior loved her more than the rest of the women.

The words of the savior, which Mary recalls at Peter's request, are as yet unknown to the disciples, and they are meant to illustrate in a more profound way the teaching of the savior to all the disciples about the child of humanity within, who is to be followed, sought after, and found. Whereas the disciples think of the child of humanity as the one who suffered, and fear their own suffering, Mary stresses his greatness, which has prepared them and made them truly human. In addition, by recalling words of the savior that she knows and the others do not, she shows the way out of their wavering. The disciples need not depend on their soul's senses, nor do they need to wait for divine inspiration from outside. The savior has explained to Mary that there are not two categories, soul and spirit, but three: soul, mind, and spirit. Their own minds, which have the spirit of the child of humanity within, enable the disciples, first, to see the master's greatness; second, to become stable; and third, to experience bliss.

After the missing pages, Mary tells the disciples what the savior taught her about how inner stability and eventually divine rest can be achieved. Whereas the disciples in their wavering are convinced that the gentiles will inflict suffering, Mary shows them the identity of the real adversaries (compare Ephesians 6:12), which are not only outside, but also inside and among the disciples. The powers of darkness, desire, ignorance, and wrath keep the soul in bondage. These opponents are, however, not to be feared, since they can be joyfully overcome. Inner stability and divine rest can be realized by identifying false reasoning with the help of divine reason, which consists of the conviction that the soul has been freed from her bondage. The false reasoning of the powers emphasizes instead that the soul still belongs to them.

The author is clear that Mary's teaching about the words of the savior is the focal point of the gospel. But the gospel does not end there. Rather, the trustworthiness of Mary as a woman is questioned. Andrew reacts quite bluntly to what "she" says: Mary's words cannot be from the savior since they seem to be at odds with what the disciples already know. Peter becomes entangled in social rules about "a woman" and men. Mary reacts strongly, and Levi tries to mediate but still excludes "the woman" from the group of disciples. The Gospel of Mary ends here, with uncertainty. Are Mary's words accepted? Is her teaching incorporated? The title shows that Mary's words are accepted by the author or an early copyist, and he or she wants the readers to embrace Mary's teaching and understand its importance. But Andrew, Peter, and even Levi seem to have decided to do without her. For them, accepting a woman as a fellow disciple and teacher is impossible.

Apparently, in the author's view, Mary is a disciple of Jesus, the savior, in the sense that she has been taught by him. She also has had access to teaching that the others have not heard. She alone has been taught by the savior about how inner stability and divine rest can be experienced, who the soul's adversaries are, and how to handle them. In addition, she has been prepared by the child of humanity to proclaim the Gospel of the kingdom and has been made a true human being, like the other disciples. Furthermore, the author gives indications that Mary, in the author's view, represents the savior after he has departed. She is able to turn the disciples' hearts inward to the child of humanity within. The author also shows how the savior regards Mary: he calls her blessed, because she endeavors to live according to her renewed mind and is going up to the divine. Mary's esteem for the savior appears from her eagerness to learn from him. She does not focus on his suffering but on his greatness, and she has seen him glorified in a vision.

In the author's view, Mary is a disciple among the disciples. After the crucifixion and the resurrection of the child of humanity, she is a special disciple, because she, as the savior's representative after his departure, has the task of persuading the disciples to go and proclaim the Gospel of the kingdom of the child of humanity. But the author shows that the position of Mary among the disciples is ambiguous. When she encourages the weeping disciples, she is accepted by them and apparently arouses their curiosity to know more about her view of the savior. But when she discloses more, she is not accepted. It is difficult to understand precisely why this is the case. What exactly makes Andrew and Peter so angry, and why does Levi hesitate to acknowledge plainly that her teaching comes from the savior?

The author signals two related problems: the content of Mary's teaching, and her place as a woman. This leads to a third problem: the relation between Mary and the savior. Would the savior as a man have taught Mary as a woman? Could she really know things that differ from what the others know? The author presents three views toward Mary among the disciples. First, Mary may be lying about the savior, since she discloses things that seem to differ from what the disciples already know; moreover, the savior, as a man, would never have told her, as a woman, things that the male disciples would need to listen to. Second, Mary may be more knowledgeable than the other disciples since the savior loved her more than the rest of the women. Third, the savior may have made Mary worthy because he knows her thoroughly; that is why he loved her more than the others.

Each of these three views is rejected by the author. Mary is not lying, nor has she, as "the woman," been made worthy, singled out by the savior because of his love and knowledge of her. In the view of the author, Mary is simply a disciple like the others, having been prepared and made truly human like them, although in her case she knows things that the others do not know and acts accordingly.

To the author, Mary's words are crucial. She is able to help the disciples turn their hearts inward, away from being concerned about the suffering of the child of humanity and the threat from "the gentiles." She points the disciples to the joyous recognition of the savior's greatness: he prepared the disciples to preach the Gospel and made them true human beings. Mary also shows the identity of the real adversaries to true humanity, the importance of the disciples' renewed minds, and the way through which inner stability and divine rest can be experienced.

Mary's teaching thus explains that, although the proclamation of the Gospel may inflict temporary suffering, the content of the Gospel is vital to the liberation, the joy and the victory of the soul. Mary's words empower the disciples to see that their fear to proclaim the Gospel is based on false reasoning and originates from the real adversaries which can be joyfully overcome. Mary Magdalene in the Gospel of Mary encourages and helps the readers to proclaim the Gospel in a hostile environment, warning them against the unexpected closeness of opposing powers of passion (such as Peter's and Andrew's striving for a male hierarchy), as well as confirming their essential freedom from passion's grip, thanks to the new identity the savior has given them.

THE NEW TESTAMENT GOSPELS

After reading the Gospel of Mary and other extracanonical texts about Mary Magdalene, a question arises: Why do the New Testament Gospels tell so little about her? It is clear that the New Testament Gospels show traces of a high esteem for Mary Magdalene, but they also show traces of a decision to reduce the importance of her role. (For a detailed exegesis of the New Testament Gospels on Mary Magdalene see de Boer, *The Gospel of Mary*.) Mark suggests that all is lost at the end of the Gospel, when Mary Magdalene, Mary of James, and Salome do not speak, (Mark 16:8). No one will go to Galilee and see the risen Jesus. With this open ending the readers themselves are strongly invited to speak, because they know that Mary Magdalene and the others eventually must have spoken, too, since they are reading their story. The readers are encouraged to overcome their fear just as Mary Magdalene, Mary of James, and Salome must have overcome theirs.

Compared with Mark, Matthew puts Mary Magdalene in a golden cage. She is no longer the important witness of Mark, on whom the impact of Jesus' work depends. To be sure, she is the faithful and courageous model disciple who experiences the opening of the tomb, meets the risen Jesus, and joyfully obeys him (Matthew 28:1–10), but the real impact of Jesus' work depends on himself and the eleven disciples (Matthew 28:16–20). Luke takes a different view. In Luke, Mary Magdalene is also special, as in Matthew, though not because of her belief and courage, but because she has been healed of seven evil spirits (Luke 8:2). Her account of the revelation at the empty tomb is not accepted, but instead causes confusion and so is deemed superfluous, whereas the word that the master has been seen by Simon is readily believed (Luke 24:1–36).

Although Matthew and Luke go in very different directions, they resemble each other, compared with Mark, in that they introduce male disciples to deemphasize the importance of Mary Magdalene. Both suggest that the impact of Jesus' work rests squarely on the shoulders of the eleven male disciples instead of on the shoulders of Mary Magdalene and the women accompanying her. On the basis of this observation, we must conclude that one of the reasons why Matthew and Luke limit the role of Mary Magdalene is that she is a woman. This is affirmed by the exclusion of women from consideration for apostleship in the Lukan account at the beginning of the Acts of the Apostles (Acts 1:22).

In this regard another observation is important as well. Although the synoptic Gospels differ considerably in their portrayals of Mary Magdalene, they are similar in that the main content of Mary Magdalene's instruction is not new to the disciples. In the synoptic Gospels Mary Magdalene and the other women first and foremost have the role of reminding the disciples of words Jesus already spoke when he was among them. In contrast to the synoptic accounts, in the account of John, the main content of the instruction entrusted to Mary Magdalene is new to the disciples (John 20:17). In addition, Mary Magdalene interprets Jesus' instruction on her own (she does not go to Jesus' brothers but to his disciples, John 20:18), and on the basis of the prologue the readers know her interpretation to be the right one (John 1:12–13). In contrast to the synoptic Gospels, John does not hesitate to depict women, like the Samaritan woman (John 4) and Martha (John 11), in dialogue with Jesus. At the same time, however, the Gospel of John and the synoptic Gospels remain androcentric. In the synoptic Gospels many women are said to follow Jesus, but these women are not depicted in dialogue with him. In John women are in dialogue with Jesus, but John portrays them within carefully defined boundaries (Martha and Mary are the sisters of Jesus' friend; Mary Magdalene is in the company of his mother; he asks the Samaritan woman to fetch her husband) and does not picture women traveling with Jesus.

In the Gospel of Mary the teaching of Mary Magdalene is openly discussed. Is she to be relied on? Do her words really come from the savior? Are the disciples to believe that the savior would have taught a woman alone and that the disciples should listen to her? This kind of discussion is not openly dealt with in the New Testament Gospels. In the New Testament Gospels, the discussion of the position of Mary Magdalene is only implicitly present. And the outcome of this discussion is very different: whereas the Gospel of Mary chooses to depict Mary Magdalene as a disciple to whom one should listen carefully, the New Testament Gospels show ambiguity and reservation with regard to her role as well as the roles of other women disciples.

At first, compared with other writings, it seems extraordinary that the author of the Gospel of Mary gives Mary Magdalene such an explicit role. I wonder, however, whether we should say something more. Is it not extraordinary that the New Testament Gospels take so much trouble to limit her role? Do they do so just because she is a woman? But we must be careful, and acknowledge that the New Testament Gospels seem to have different reasons for keeping Mary Magdalene silent.

The common themes about Mary Magdalene in the New Testament Gospels provide evidence of first-century traditions about her. But if she was generally known as a disciple of Jesus and closely related to the circumstances that led to the core confession of the first Christians, then we can imagine that there must have been stories not only about her presence at Jesus' crucifixion and his grave but also about what she learned from him and the content of her Gospel.

Mark may have made use of these stories, but we do not know for sure, since Mark has its own theological purpose. The Gospel of Mark identifies only the twelve apostles by name, and does not directly identify any disciple, but consistently uses an unspecified plural to refer to the disciples as an open invitation to the readers to become disciples themselves.[20] Mark portrays Mary Magdalene, the other two Marys, and Salome at the end of the Gospel, contrasting them to the Twelve, to reveal what discipleship actually means. In Mark 15:40–41, it turns out that the disciples who truly understand what following Jesus means are not the specified male Twelve, who thought themselves to be the authorized followers of Jesus (Mark 9:30–40; 10:32–45), but who in fact betrayed him (Judas), denied him (Peter) and ran away when he was arrested. Instead, the until then unknown and implied women followers at this point of Mark's story illustrate that discipleship has nothing to do with power, but with the utmost willingness to follow and to remain of service, even when it is dangerous to do so, which Mark emphasizes by situating the women looking on from afar.[21] In addition, Mary Magdalene's, Mary's and Salome's portrayal as those who remain silent has a literary focus, challenging the readers to overcome their own silence.[22]

In the Gospel of Matthew no explicit role of Mary Magdalene as a disciple is required, since the author presents Jesus' disciples first and foremost as the twelve males. To them the readers should turn, to be made disciples, to be baptized, and to be taught. The Gospel of Luke seems to address the issue of gender, though subtly. Luke's gender pairs, parallel stories with respectively a woman and a man as subject (e.g. the shepherd with his lost sheep and the woman with her lost coin, in Luke 15:3–7; 8–10), convey a picture of a world divided by gender.[23] Luke speaks favorably of women when their strength and perseverance are concerned with hearing the word of God and doing it, with prayer, and with the sharing of possessions (e.g. Luke 11:27–28; 18:1–8; Acts 9:36), but he also uses the narrative technique of silencing them. Luke regularly introduces women whom the readers are supposed to imagine speaking, but who at the same time are silenced, since Luke grants them no actual voice (e.g. the prophetess Anna in Luke 2:36–38 and the woman who had suffered from severe bleeding in Luke 8:47). The witness of the Galilean women, Mary Magdalene among them, is unimportant, except for the women themselves.

The Gospel of John shows a different motive. According to the author of the fourth Gospel, Mary Magdalene's interpretation and proclamation of the meaning of Jesus' death, resurrection, and ascension are authoritative. In addition, other teachings of Mary Magdalene as an eyewitness may also be present in John, but there are conservative boundaries to be dealt with. In the Gospel of John, even Jesus himself only gradually comes to the understanding that women may be sowers of the seed, and that the disciples should not be afraid, and should not hinder them, but may rejoice with them, reaping the harvest (John 4).

All of this marginalizing of Mary Magdalene, while not eliminating her, forcefully reveals that she was a crucial disciple of Jesus with her own distinct role and Gospel. The balancing of the Gospel of Mary and the other non-canonical texts against the New Testament's "official" minimalizing allows Mary finally to emerge from the shadows of history.

Notes

Introduction

1. See Jerome, Epistle 127, discussed by Esther de Boer, below.
2. Cf. Marvin Meyer, *Secret Gospels*, 107–78.

Chapter One

1. On the Gospel of John and the Song of Songs, cf. Susanne Ruschmann, *Maria von Magdala im Johannesevangelium*, 201–7.
2. These translations of selections from the Gospels of Mark, Matthew, Luke, John, and Peter are based on the critical Greek texts of these Gospels. For the Gospel of Peter, see Albert Fuchs, *Das Petrusevangelium* (Linz: F. Plochl, 1978); Maria Grazia Mara, *Évangile de Pierre* (Paris: Cerf, 1973); Henry Barclay Swete, *The Apocryphal Gospel of Peter* (London: Macmillan, 1893).
3. In the preceding passage (Luke 7:36–50) the story is told of an unnamed woman, said to be a sinner, who washes Jesus' feet with her tears, dries them with her hair, and kisses them and anoints them with myrrh. See the additional stories of women around Jesus.
4. Cf. Mark 16:9 (the longer ending of Mark).
5. Luke claims that Joanna, one of the independent women traveling with Jesus and providing support, is the wife of one of Herod's officials, Chuza, who is a steward or manager (*epitropos*) of Herod. Since, according to Luke, she seems to be traveling without Chuza, Joanna may be separated or divorced from Chuza, she may be gone with or without Chuza's consent, or she may be a widow. Joanna is also mentioned in Luke 24:10.

6.   Susanna is said to be another of the independent women traveling with Jesus.

7.   The Greek verb used here and translated "supported" is a form of *diakonein*, which means "to provide *diakonia*, service, support, assistance."

8.   Some ancient texts, including Codex Sinaiticus, read "him"—i.e., Jesus.

9.   Midday on Friday.

10.   Cf. Ps. 22:2; Matt. 27:46; Pet. 5:5. Mark has Jesus cite Psalm 22 in Aramaic, Matthew has Jesus cite the Psalm in Hebrew ("Eli, Eli . . ."), and Peter has Jesus say, "My power, O power, you have abandoned me."

11.   Mary of Clopas, probably the wife of Clopas, may be a relative, even a sister, of Mary the mother of Jesus, but she remains an elusive character. If Clopas is identical with Cleopas in Luke 24:18, then Mary the wife of Clopas could be the unnamed second disciple of Jesus on the road to Emmaus, in Luke's account. Compare also Mary the mother of James (or the mother of James and Joses [or Joseph]), and "the other Mary." Equally uncertain is the identity of the person described as "his mother's sister" just before. She may be the same person as Mary of Clopas.

12.   On the beloved disciple in the Gospel of John and elsewhere, see the general introduction.

13.   Jesus here refers either to the beloved disciple or to himself as Mary's son. See the general introduction.

14.   Salome is a disciple of Jesus described as being present at the crucifixion in this passage and at the tomb in Mark 16:1. In Gospel of Thomas 61 Jesus is said to have climbed onto Salome's couch (or "bed") and to have eaten from her table, and Salome declares that she is a disciple of Jesus. She is also featured throughout Pistis Sophia and in Manichaean texts, including the Psalms of Heracleides.

15.   Cf. Joses. In the textual tradition of Matthew there are several different readings here.

16.   In Luke 23:49 no women are named, and reference is simply made to acquaintances of Jesus and the women who followed him from Galilee.

17.   Later on Friday.

18.   Joseph of Arimathea, a member of the Sanhedrin, is mentioned elsewhere in early Christian literature (e.g., Matt. 27:57, 59; Luke 23:50; John 19:38). He is also a character in the Gospel of Peter, and in Pet. 2:1 he is described as a friend of both Jesus and Pilate.

19.   "The other Mary" may be the same person as Mary the mother of James and Joses (or Joseph).

20.   In Luke 23:55–56 the women from Galilee follow, observe, and prepare spices, but no names are given.

21. In Greek, *mathêtria*, "woman disciple."

22. The Gospel of Peter, like other Christian texts, can express polemical sentiments against the Jewish leaders and the Jewish people, in spite of the historical fact that Jesus, Mary Magdalene, and all the disciples were Jewish.

23. Cf. Matt. 27:61.

24. In Luke 24:1 the unnamed women come to the tomb, and soon thereafter they see two men in bright clothing, who tell them that Christ has risen from the dead.

25. The Greek for "youth" is *neaniskos*, and the figure is not depicted as a heavenly angel. Cf. also the *neaniskos* in Mark 14:51–52 and in the Secret Gospel of Mark. Conversely, in Matthew there is an apocalyptic angel, in Luke two men in dazzling clothes (with a report of "a vision of angels"), and in John two messengers or angels dressed in white.

26. Most scholars conclude that originally the Gospel of Mark ended here, at 16:8.

27. Or, "Be joyful."

28. The twelve disciples without Judas Iscariot.

29. Cf. Luke 8:1–3.

30. Cf. also the longer ending of the Gospel of Mark.

31. The longer ending of the Gospel of Mark is thought by most scholars to be a later addition to Mark.

32. Cf. Luke 8:2.

33. On the beloved disciple (here equated with "the other disciple") in the Gospel of John and elsewhere, see the general introduction. If the beloved disciple is understood to be Mary Magdalene, then the tension here between Peter and the beloved disciple may be reminiscent of the conflict between Peter and Mary in the Gospel of Mary, the Gospel of Thomas, and Pistis Sophia.

34. Or "angels" (Greek, *angeloi*).

35. On this story of Mary searching for and finding Jesus, cf. Song of Songs 3:1–5.

36. "Rabbouni" (or "Rabboni") means "rabbi" or "my rabbi"; "my dear rabbi" may also be possible. "Rabbi" means "master" or "lord"; here in John the meaning "teacher" is suggested.

37. In Greek, *mê mou haptou*. The Greek verb *haptein* can mean "touch," "handle," "hold on to," or "have sex with," so that this command not to touch Jesus could suggest several possible interpretations.

38. Myrrh was a precious perfume, sometimes used for embalming, so this word may be translated "perfume," here and below.

39. Perhaps compare Simon the leper in Mark 14:1–9.

40. A denarius was a Roman silver coin worth about what might be paid for a typical day's labor.

41. Perhaps compare Simon the Pharisee in Luke 7:36–50.

42. Three hundred denarii would be about a year's wages.

43. Matt. 26:6–13 presents a very similar story of the woman who anointed Jesus at Bethany.

44. About a year's wages.

CHAPTER TWO

1. This translation of the Gospel of Mary is based primarily on the Coptic text in *Nag Hammadi Codices V,2–5 and VI with Papyrus Berolinensis 8502,1 and 4*, ed. Douglas M. Parrott (Leiden: E. J. Brill, 1979), 453–71; the Greek texts of Papyrus Oxyrhynchus 3525 and Papyrus Rylands 463 have also been consulted, along with the translations of Esther A. de Boer, *The Gospel of Mary: Beyond a Gnostic and a Biblical Mary Magdalene* (London: T & T Clark [Continuum], 2004), and Karen L. King, *The Gospel of Mary of Magdala: Jesus and the First Woman Apostle* (Santa Rosa, CA: Polebridge, 2003).

2. The first six pages are missing from the Coptic manuscript, and the extant text begins in the middle of a dialogue between Jesus and his disciples on the nature of matter.

3. Cf. Gospel of Philip 53.

4. Lit. "act adulterously."

5. In the Gospel of Mary adultery is understood to be improper mingling with the world. Cf. the similar perspective in the Exegesis on the Soul, from the Nag Hammadi library, Heracleon's Commentary on the Gospel of John, and Gospel of Philip 61.

6. Cf. the discussion of sin in Romans 7.

7. Cf. Luke 24:38; John 14:27.

8. Or "images of nature." On truth being present in symbols and images, cf. Gospel of Philip 67.

9. Cf. John 14:27; 20:19, 21, 26.

10. Or, "son of man," here and below.

11. Cf. Luke 17:21; Gospel of Thomas 113.

12. Or "him," here and in the next sentence.

13. The departure of Jesus could be either his crucifixion or his resurrection and ascension.

14. Most likely Mary Magdalene, throughout the text, since this portrayal of Mary resembles Mary Magdalene as presented elsewhere.

15. In Papyrus Oxyrhynchus 3525 it is added that Mary also kissed them tenderly.

16. Or, perhaps, with Karen King, "brothers and sisters," here and below, though no other women are mentioned in the text.

17. On the special love of Jesus for Mary Magdalene, see below, Gospel of Mary 17–18, as well as Gospel of Philip 59; 63–64; also Pistis Sophia 17; 19.

18. Here Karen King, *The Gospel of Mary of Magdala*, 196, suggests that the Greek of Papyrus Oxyrhynchus 3525 may imply that Jesus appeared more than once ("*Once* when the Lord appeared to me in a vision. . . .").

19. Cf. Matt. 6:21.

20. Pp. 11–14 are missing from the Coptic manuscript. The text resumes as Mary is recounting her vision of the ascent of the soul beyond the cosmic powers. The vision apparently described four stages of ascent, and these stages may have depicted the liberation of the soul from the four elements of this world. The name of the first power is missing from the text, but it may have been "darkness," according to the list of the forms of the fourth power. The names of the others powers are "desire," "ignorance," and, apparently, "wrath," a deadly composite power. As in other texts relating to gnostic religion and the career of the soul, the soul ascends through the realms of the powers and is interrogated by them. The soul is successful in her ascent from this world of matter and body, and she is set free at last. Cf. also Gospel of Thomas 50.

21. This garment, which clothes the soul, is made up of all the features that characterize bodily existence in this world. The soul puts on this garment upon entering the world and takes it off when leaving the world.

22. Compare the seven heavenly spheres (often for the sun, moon, and five planets) described by ancient astronomers and astrologers. On the names of the seven powers of wrath, compare the Secret Book of John.

23. Or "from," here and later in the sentence.

24. On the hostility of Peter toward Mary Magdalene, cf. Gospel of Thomas 114; Pistis Sophia 36; 72; 146.

25. Levi was a disciple of Jesus, named Levi son of Alphaeus in the Gospel of Mark and said to be a tax collector from Capernaum. Sometimes (cf. Matt. 9:9; 10:3) Levi is identified with the disciple Matthew, but the identification is uncertain. (In the Dialogue of the Savior, Matthew is one of the three main disciples with whom Jesus is in dialogue.)

26. On the love of Jesus for Mary, see above, Gospel of Mary 10, and Gospel of Philip 59; 63–64; Pistis Sophia 17; 19.

27. Or "nurture."

28. In Papyrus Rylands 463 only Levi is said to leave in order to preach.

Chapter Three

1. This translation of portions of the Gospel of Thomas is based on an ultraviolet collation of the Coptic text, by Marvin Meyer, at the Coptic Museum in 1988; see Marvin Meyer, *The Gospel of Thomas* (San Francisco: HarperCollins, 1992), for text and translation. Cf. also the text and translation in the corrected printing of the appendix by the Berliner Arbeitskreis für koptisch-gnostische Schriften, "Das Thomas-Evangelium / The Gospel According to Thomas," in *Synopsis Quattuor Evangeliorum*, ed. Kurt Aland (Stuttgart: Deutsche Bibelgesellschaft, 1996), 517–46.

2. Didymos.

3. Cf. Secret Book of James 2; Book of Thomas 138.

4. Probably Jesus, possibly Judas Thomas.

5. Cf. Sir. 39:1–3; John 8:51–52.

6. Papyrus 654.8–9 adds "and [having reigned], one will rest." For the saying in general cf. Gospel of the Hebrews 4a, 4b; Book of Thomas 140–41; 145; Matt. 7:7–8 (Q); Luke 11:9–10 (Q); Dialogue of the Savior 20; Wisdom of Solomon 6:12, 17–20.

7. Papyrus Oxyrhynchus 654.13 reads "under the earth."

8. Cf. Luke 17:20–21; Gospel of Thomas 113; Manichaean Psalmbook 160.

9. "Know yourself" was among the Greek inscriptions at Delphi. On knowing and being known, cf. Gal. 4:8–9; 1 Cor. 8:1–3, 13:12; Gospel of Truth 19.

10. Probably an uncircumcised child (Jewish boys were circumcised on the eighth day).

11. Cf. Hippolytus, *Refutation of All Heresies* 5.7.20, a saying said to derive from the Gospel of Thomas: "One who seeks will find me in children from seven years, for there, hidden in the fourteenth age, I am revealed."

12. Cf. Matt. 20:16 (Q); Luke 13:30 (Q); Matt. 19:30; Mark 10:31; Barnabas 6:13; Pistis Sophia 87. Here Papyrus Oxyrhynchus 654.25–26 reads "For many of the [first] will be [last, and] the last first."

13. Cf. Manichaean Kephalaia 65 163,26–29.

14. Cf. Mark 4:22; Luke 8:17; Matt. 10:26 (Q); Luke 12:2 (Q). On the last portion of the saying, cf. Gospel of Thomas 6. Papyrus Oxyrhynchus 654.31 adds "and nothing buried that [will not be raised]."

15. Cf. Matt. 6:1–18; Didache 8:1–3. Saying 14 provides a more direct answer to these questions.

16. This is the negative formulation of the golden rule.

17. Papyrus Oxyrhynchus 654.38 reads "truth" (Greek *alêtheia*, equivalent to Coptic *me*; here the Coptic for "heaven" is *pe*).

18. Cf. Gospel of Thomas 5.

19. Or "foul."

20. Here the lion seems to symbolize what is passionate and bestial in human experience. A person may consume the lion or be consumed by it. Cf. Plato, *Republic* 588E–589B.

21. Or "The human," "The man."

22. Cf. Matt. 13:47–50; Babrius, Fable 4.

23. Cf. Matt. 13:3–9; Mark 4:2–9; Luke 8:4–8.

24. Cf. Luke 12:49 (Q ?) ; Pistis Sophia 141.

25. Cf. Matt. 24:35; Mark 13:31; Luke 21:33; Matt. 5:18 (Q); Luke 16:17 (Q).

26. Cf. Hippolytus, *Refutation of All Heresies* 5.8.32: "So they say, 'If you ate dead things and made them living, what will you do if you eat living things?'"

27. Or "angel."

28. Or "three words." The three sayings or words are unknown, and they may be mentioned as a device to provoke the creative reflection of the reader.

29. Cf. Gospel of Bartholomew 2:5.

30. Cf. the questions in Gospel of Thomas 6.

31. Literally, "walk in the places."

32. Cf. Matt. 10:8 (Q); Luke 10:8–9 (Q); 1 Cor. 10:27.

33. Cf. Matt. 15:11; Mark 7:15.

34. Cf. John 10:30.

35. Cf. Matt. 10:34–36 (Q); Luke 12:49 (Q ?), 50, 51–53 (Q).

36. Cf. 1 Cor. 2:9; Isa. 64:4; Apocalypse of Elijah or Secrets (Apocrypha) of Elijah; Dialogue of the Savior 140; Plutarch, *How the Young Person Should Study Poetry* 17E.

37. Cf. Matt. 24:3; Mark 13:3–4; Luke 21:7.

38. Cf. Gospel of Thomas 49.

39. Cf. Gospel of Philip 64; Lactantius, *Divine Institutes* 4.8; Irenaeus, *Proof of the Apostolic Preaching* 43.

40. Cf., e.g., Gospel of Thomas 77.

41. Five trees in paradise are mentioned elsewhere in gnostic and Manichaean literature. Cf. Gen. 2:9.

42. Cf. Matt. 13:31–32 (Q); Luke 13:18–19 (Q); Mark 4:30–32.

43. Mary Magdalene? Some other Mary? Cf. Gospel of Thomas 114.

44. The editors of "Das Thomas-Evangelium / The Gospel According to Thomas," in *Synopsis Quattuor Evangeliorum*, ed. Kurt Aland (Stuttgart: Deutsche Bibelgesellschaft, 1996), translate this passage as follows: "They are like servants entrusted with a field that is not theirs" (525).

45. Cf. Gospel of Thomas 37.

46. Cf. Gospel of Thomas 103; Matt. 24:43 (Q); Luke 12:39 (Q).

47. Cf. Mark 4:29; Joel 3:13.

48. Cf. Gal. 3:27–28; Gospel of the Egyptians 5; 2 Clement 12:2–6; Martyrdom of Peter 9; Acts of Philip 140. For another saying on transformation that employs gender categories in a rather different way, cf. Gospel of Thomas 114.

49. This saying recalls the accounts of the career of the soul or of the person in the Secret Book of John, the Hymn of the Pearl, and the Exegesis on the Soul. On the soul being interrogated by the cosmic powers and ascending to the realm above, cf. Gospel of Mary 15–17.

50. Cf. Luke 17:20–21; Gospel of Thomas 113; John 3:18–19; 5:25; 2 Tim. 2:17–18; Treatise on Resurrection 49.

51. 2 Esd. 14:45 gives twenty-four as the number of books in the Jewish scriptures.

52. Cf. Augustine, *Against the Adversary of the Law and the Prophets* 2.4.14.

53. Cf. Rom. 2:25–29.

54. Cf. Matt. 5:3 (Q); Luke 6:20 (Q).

55. Cf. Matt. 10:37–38 (Q); Luke 14:26–27 (Q); Matt. 16:24; Mark 8:34; Luke 9:23; Gospel of Thomas 101; Manichaean Psalmbook 175.25–30.

56. Cf. Luke 17:34–35 (Q); Matt. 24:40–41 (Q).

57. Salome is a disciple of Jesus described as being present at the crucifixion in Mark 15:40 and at the tomb in Mark 16:1. She is also featured throughout Pistis Sophia and Manichaean texts.

58. Or "bed."

59. Literally, "as from one." The editors of "Das Thomas-Evangelium / The Gospel According to Thomas," in *Synopsis Quattuor Evangeliorum*, ed. Kurt Aland (Stuttgart: Deutsche Bibelgesellschaft, 1996), suggest that the text should be emended, and they opt for the translation "as a <stranger>" (534).

60. Cf. Matt. 11:27 (Q); Luke 10:22 (Q); John 3:35; 6:37–39; 13:3–4.

61. Here the word for "disciple" is *mathêtês*, a word of Greek origin.

62. Cf. John 8:12.

63. Cf. Matt. 9:37–38 (Q); Luke 10:2 (Q); Pirke Avot 2.20.

64. Literally, "He said."

65. Also possible is the reading "<well>."

66. Or "no one."

67. Sayings 73–75 most likely constitute a small dialogue. Cf. "Heavenly Dialogue," in Origen, *Against Celsus* 8:15. For saying 75, cf. Matt. 25:1–13. The wedding chamber or bridal chamber is discussed extensively in the Gospel of Philip.

68. Cf. Matt. 13:45–46.

69. Cf. Matt. 6:19–20 (Q); Luke 12:33 (Q); Matt. 13:44.

70. Cf. John 8:12; Wisd. of Sol. 7:24–30.

71. Cf. Rom. 11:36; 1 Cor. 8:6; Martyrdom of Peter 10.

72. Cf. Eccles. 10:9; Hab. 2:18–20; Lucian of Samosata, *Hermotimus* 81.

73. Cf. Matt. 11:7–8 (Q); Luke 7:24–25 (Q).

74. Cf. Luke 11:27–28 (Q ?); Petronius, *Satyricon* 94.

75. Cf. John 13:17; James 1:25.

76. Cf. Luke 23:29; Matt. 24:19; Mark 13:17; Luke 21:23; Gospel of the Egyptians 3.

77. Cf. Gospel of Thomas 56.

78. Cf. 1 Cor. 4:8; Gospel of Thomas 110; Dialogue of the Savior 20.

79. Cf. Gospel of the Savior; Ignatius, *Smyrnaeans* 4:2; Greek proverbs. Versions of this saying are also known from Origen, Didymus the Blind, and an Armenian text from the Monastery of St. Lazzaro.

80. For sayings 83–84 cf. Gen. 1:26–28 and discussions in Philo of Alexandria and gnostic accounts of creation.

81. Simon Magus was called the great power of God. Cf. Acts 8:9–10; Concept of Our Great Power.

82. Cf. Matt. 8:20 (Q); Luke 9:58 (Q); Plutarch, *Life of Tiberius Gracchus* 9.4–5; Abu Hamid Muhammad al-Ghazali, *Revival of the Religious Sciences* 3.153. "Child of humanity" may also be translated "son of man," and here the phrase is used by Jesus as a general reference to a person or even as a reference to himself.

83. Cf. Gospel of Thomas 29; 112.

84. Or "angels."

85. Cf. Secret Book of John II 25; Authoritative Teaching 32.

86. Cf. Matt. 23:25–26 (Q); Luke 11:39–41 (Q); Babylonian Talmud, Berakoth 51a; Kelim 25.1–9.

87. Cf. Matt. 11:28–30; Sir. 51:26–27.

88. Cf. Matt. 16:1, 2–3 (Q); Luke 12:54–56 (Q).

89. Cf. Gospel of Thomas 2; 94; Matt. 7:7–8 (Q); Luke 11:9–10 (Q).

90. Cf. John 16:4–5, 12–15, 22–28; song from the Manichaean Psalms of Heracleides (Manichaean Psalmbook 187, below).

91. Cf. Matt. 7:6. Bentley Layton, *Nag Hammadi Codex II,2–7* (Leiden: E. J. Brill, 1989), notes the following additional suggestions for restoration: "or they might grind it [to bits]"; "or they might bring it [to naught]" (1:86–87).

92. Cf. Gospel of Thomas 2; 92; Matt. 7:7–8 (Q); Luke 11:9–10 (Q).

93. Cf. Matt. 5:42 (Q); Luke 6:30 (Q), 34–35b (Q ?), 35c (Q); Didache 1:5.

94. Cf. Matt. 13:33 (Q); Luke 13:20–21 (Q).

95. This parable is known only here in early Christian literature, though a somewhat similar story is found in "Macarius" of Syria.

96. This parable is known only here in early Christian literature. In general cf. Gospel of Thomas 35; Matt. 11:12–13 (Q); Luke 16:16 (Q).

97. Cf. Matt. 12:46–50; Mark 3:31–35; Luke 8:19–21; Gospel of the Ebionites 5.

98. Cf. Matt. 22:15–22; Mark 12:13–17; Luke 20:20–26.

99. This restoration remains tentative. Another possible restoration: "For my mother, who has [given birth to me, has destroyed me]" (see the note in *Synopsis Quattuor Evangeliorum*, ed. Kurt Aland [Stuttgart: Deutsche Bibelgesellschaft, 1996], 543). It is also possible, though more difficult, to restore to read the entire sentence as follows: "For my mother [gave birth to me], but my true [mother] gave life to me."

100. Perhaps the holy spirit as spiritual mother; cf. Gospel of the Hebrews 3; Secret Book of James 6; Gospel of Philip 55.

101. Cf. Matt. 10:37–38 (Q); Luke 12:26–27 (Q); Gospel of Thomas 55.

102. Cf. Matt. 23:13 (Q); Luke 11:52 (Q); Gospel of Thomas 39; Aesop, Fable 702.

103. Cf. Gospel of Thomas 21; Matt. 24:43 (Q); Luke 12:39 (Q).

104. Cf. Matt. 9:14–15; Mark 2:18–20; Luke 5:33–35; Gospel of the Nazoreans 2. The wedding chamber or bridal chamber is discussed extensively in the Gospel of Philip.

105. On despising physical connections, cf. Gospel of Thomas 55; 101; Book of Thomas 144. On Simon Magus, Helena, and the soul's prostitution, cf. Irenaeus, *Against Heresies* 1.23.2; Exegesis on the Soul. On the tradition of Jesus as the illegitimate child of Mary, cf. Origen, *Against Celsus* 1.28, 32; perhaps John 8:41.

106. Cf. Gospel of Thomas 48; Matt. 18:19; 17:20b (Q); Luke 17:6b (Q); Matt. 21:21; Mark 11:23; 1 Cor. 13:2.

107. Cf. Matt. 18:12–13 (Q); Luke 15:4–7 (Q); Ezek. 34:15–16.

108. Cf. Gospel of Thomas 13; John 4:13–14; 7:37–39; 1 Cor. 10:1–4; Sir. 24:21.

109. Cf. Prov. 2:1–5; Sir. 20:30–31; Matt. 13:44; Midrash Rabbah, Song of Songs 4.12.1; Aesop, Fable 42.

110. Cf. Gospel of Thomas 27; 81.

111. Cf. Isa. 34:4; Ps. 102:25–27; (some ancient texts); Heb. 1:10–12; Rev. 6:13–14.

112. This may be a later comment incorporated into the saying.

113. Cf. Gospel of Thomas 29; 87.

114. Or "They will not say."

115. Cf. Mark 13:21–23; Matt. 24:23–25, 26–27 (Q); Luke 17:20–22, 23–24 (Q); Gospel of Thomas 3; Gospel of Mary 8.

116. On the conflict between Peter and Mary (almost certainly Mary Magdalene, since this portrayal of Mary resembles Mary Magdalene as presented elsewhere), cf. Gospel of Mary 17–18; Pistis Sophia 36; 72; 146. Here the female may symbolize what is earthly and perishable and the male what is heavenly and imperishable. Cf. Hippolytus, *Refutation of All Heresies* 5.8.44; Clement of Alexandria, *Excerpts from Theodotus* 79; First Apocalypse of James 41; Zostrianos 131. For another saying on transformation that employs gender categories in a different manner, cf. Gospel of Thomas 22.

CHAPTER FOUR

1. This translation of portions of the Gospel of Philip is based on the Coptic text in *Nag Hammadi Codex II,2–7*, ed. Bentley Layton (Leiden: E. J. Brill, 1989), 1:129–217, which has been read in the light of other editions. Other translations consulted include Willis Barnstone and Marvin Meyer, *The Gnostic Bible* (Boston: Shambhala, 2003); Bentley Layton, *The Gnostic Scriptures* (Garden City, NY: Doubleday, 1987), 325–53; Jacques É. Ménard, *L'Évangile selon Philippe* (Strasbourg and Paris: Letouzey & Ané, 1967); Hans-Martin Schenke, "Das Evangelium nach Philippus," in *Nag Hammadi Deutsch. I. Band*, ed. Hans-Martin Schenke, Hans-Gebhard Bethge, and Ursula Ulrike Kaiser (Berlin and New York: Walter de Gruyter, 2001), 183–213; and Hans-Martin Schenke, "The Gospel of Philip" in *New Testament Apocrypha*, ed. Wilhelm Schneemelcher (Cambridge: James Clarke; Louisville: Westminster/John Knox, 1991–92), 1:179–208. A number of the textual restorations incorporated here derive from these editions, and particularly from the translations of Hans-Martin Schenke.

2. Or "the dead will not die and will live all the more." Cf. Gospel of Thomas 11.

3. Cf. Gospel of Thomas 99; 101; 105.

4. Cf. Gospel of Thomas 14.

5. Cf. Gospel of Thomas 57.

6. Lit., "brothers," or more generally, "are related to one another."

7. Cf. Gospel of Mary 7.

8. Or "words," here and below.

9. In gnostic texts the forces are among the rulers of this world. Here they are identified with the ancient gods and goddesses, to whom sacrifices were made.

10. Ancient gods and goddesses were often depicted as animals.

11. Perhaps humankind in general, or perhaps Christ.

12. Cf. John 6:31, 50–51; Exod. 16:4; Ps. 78:23–24.

13. Or "the realm of all."

14. Cf. Matt. 1:18; 20; Luke 1:35.

15. In Hebrew and other Semitic traditions the word for "spirit" is feminine in gender, and the spirit may be considered to be the divine mother. Cf. Secret Book of James 6; Gospel of Thomas 101; esp. Gospel of the Hebrews 3, in which Jesus refers to his mother the holy spirit.

16. Matt. 16:17. Cf. also Matt. 6:9; Luke 11:2 (the Lord's Prayer).

17. Lit., "brothers."

18. The Coptic text reads "her sister" here, and the text is emended on the basis of the later reference to "his sister." On the sisters of Jesus, cf. Mark 3:32; 6:3; Matt. 13:56; in the History of Joseph the Carpenter the sisters of Jesus are named Lysia or Assia and Lydia; in Epiphanius of Salamis they are named Mary or Anna and Salome. If the first reference in the Coptic text is not emended (and the later reference is emended to read "<her> sister"), this person could be the sister of Mary the mother of Jesus; cf. John 19:25, and the note (above).

19. Here Mary Magdalene is called the *koinônos* (in the first instance, with a word of Greek origin) or the *hôtre* (in the second instance, with a word of Egyptian origin), the companion, partner, or consort of Jesus. On the love of Jesus for Mary Magdalene, cf. also Gospel of Philip 63–64.

20. This may be a reference to the father and the son, in contrast to the spirit, mentioned next, or it may be a reference to the spirit, or even to father, son, and spirit together.

21. Or "Sophia," here and below.

22. Cf. Lev. 2:13; Mark 9:49 (with the variant reading); Col. 4:6.

23. The suggested restoration, which is tentative, includes a possible reference to Lot's wife.

24. This passage seems to reflect the Valentinian distinction between a higher wisdom (often called Sophia) and a lower wisdom (often called Achamoth).

25. Adam.

26. Cain.

27. Such gnostic texts as the Secret Book of John and the Reality of the Rulers describe how the ruler of this world, sometimes with his powers, seduced or raped Eve and thus produced Cain.

28. Abel.

29. Cf. Gospel of Mary 7.

30. Or "baptizes."

31. Or "baptized."

32. For another meditation on dyeing, cf. Gospel of Philip 63.

33. The text suggests an eschatological perspective with a present realization of spiritual union with Christ and an anticipation of the future union with the father. Such an eschatological perspective is also found in the letters of Paul.

34. Compare the discussion of faith and love in 1 Corinthians 13 and Secret Book of James 8.

35. The Greek word *nazôraios* can indicate someone from Nazareth or someone who is an observant Jewish Christian.

36. The Greek word *nazarênos* indicates someone from Nazareth.

37. In Greek *christos* means "anointed."

38. In Syriac *mshiha* can have both meanings.

39. "Jesus" comes from the Hebrew and Aramaic names Yeshua and Yehoshua (Joshua), which mean "The Lord (Yahweh) is salvation" (or the like).

40. Schenke, "Gospel of Philip," 194, emends to read "<the man of> the truth."

41. I.e., "truth" and "redemption."

42. Or "spirit," here and below.

43. Jesus was "spread out" on the cross.

44. Seventy-two is a traditional number of nations in the world according to Jewish lore.

45. For another meditation on dyeing, see Gospel of Philip 61.

46. Or "Sophia."

47. Or, dividing the sentences differently, "Wisdom, who is called barren, is the mother of the angels and the companion of the [savior]. The [savior loved] Mary Magdalene. . . ." Here the word for "companion" is *koinônos*.

48. On the special love of Jesus for Mary Magdalene, cf. Gospel of Mary 10; 17–18; also Pistis Sophia 17; 19. On Mary Magdalene as the companion, partner, or consort of Jesus, cf. Gospel of Philip 59, and on kissing and conceiving by kissing, cf. Gospel of Philip 58–59.

49. On the blind person in darkness, cf. Gospel of Thomas 34.

50. Cf. Gospel of Thomas 19.

51. The reference is to baptism.

52. Or "bridegroom."

53. Probably the name "Christian."

54. Jesus.

55. Cf. Gospel of Thomas 22.

56. Perhaps cf. Gospel of Thomas 11.

57. Lit., "what is outside the outer."

58. Matt. 8:12; 22:13; 25:30.

59. Matt. 6:6.

60. Christ brings people from the material world back to the realm of fullness.

61. Emended. The Coptic text may read, without emendation, "If he again becomes complete and attains his former self, death will cease to be." This meditation suggests that death will be undone in the oneness of androgyny.

62. Matt. 27:46 and Mark 15:34, citing Ps. 22:1.

63. Or "bridal chamber," here and below.

64. Cf. Matt. 15:27; Mark 7:28.

CHAPTER FIVE

1. This translation of a portion of the Dialogue of the Savior is based on the Coptic text in *Nag Hammadi Codex III,5: The Dialogue of the Savior*, ed. Stephen Emmel (Leiden: E. J. Brill, 1984). Other translations consulted include Beate Blatz and Einar Thomassen, "The Dialogue of the Savior," in *New Testament Apocrypha*, ed. Wilhelm Schneemelcher (Cambridge: James Clarke; Louisville: Westminster/John Knox, 1991–92), 1:300–12; and Silke Petersen and Hans-Gebhard Bethge, "Der Dialog des Erlösers," in *Nag Hammadi Deutsch. 1. Band*, ed. Hans-Martin Schenke, Hans-Gebhard Bethge, and Ursula Ulrike Kaiser (Berlin and New York: Walter de Gruyter, 2001), 381–97. Some of the textual restorations incorporated here come from these editions, and particularly from "Der Dialog des Erlösers."

2. The three disciples here are most likely Judas Thomas, Matthew, and Mary Magdalene. On Judas Thomas, cf. Gospel of Thomas Prologue; 13; Book of Thomas 138. On Matthew, cf. the disciple Matthew throughout early Christian literature (as well as Matthias and Mathaias); Gospel of Thomas 13; Book of Thomas 138. On Mary, cf. Mary Magdalene as presented in the other texts in this book.

3. In Coptic (and Greek), *logos*. On the role of the word or Logos, and Jesus as the incarnate word, compare John 1 and gnostic texts. In the Gospel of John, as here, the word descends from the realm above, comes to this world below, and acts in a salvific manner. Here, in a more fully gnostic way, the word attends to the seed of light that has fallen from above and has come to be in deficiency, and returns it to the realm of the majesty.

4. Or "son of man," here and below.

5. These references to seed, power, and deficiency are typical in gnostic texts. Frequently in gnostic texts it is said that the seed of light derives from the fall of mother Sophia ("wisdom"), and the light loses some of its divine brightness and power and becomes deficient in this world below, until it is returned to the realm of the divine. Then the divine and the seed of light—i.e., people of light and knowledge—are saved and enjoy the fullness of enlightenment again. Such themes and terms recur in the Dialogue of the Savior.

6. On garments clothing the soul, and on putting on perfect humanity as a garment, cf. Gospel of Mary 15; 18. On garments of light and life given to those who enter the bridal chamber, cf. Dialogue of the Savior 138–39.

7. For similarly mystical statements cf. Gospel of Thomas 77; 108.

8. The region of deficiency is this world below, where the light is obscured in darkness.

9. The rulers or archons are the cosmic bureaucrats who govern this world on behalf of the demiurge or creator of this world. While they seem powerful and act with arrogance and bravado, they are destined to be overcome by the people of light and knowledge. Cf. 1 Cor. 6:3. The bridal chamber is discussed extensively in the Gospel of Philip; cf. also Gospel of Thomas 75.

10. On the garments of the soul and the garments of light and life, cf. Dialogue of the Savior 136–37; Gospel of Mary 15; 18.

11. Cf. Dialogue of the Savior 145.

12. Cf. Matt. 6:34.

13. Cf. Matt. 10:10 (Q); Luke 10:7 (Q); 1 Tim. 5:18.

14. Cf. Matt. 10:25. If this third saying is emended by adding a negation ("Disciples do <not> resemble their teachers"; cf. Petersen and Bethge, "Der Dialog des Erlösers," 394), then cf. John 13:16. Here in the Dialogue of the Savior it is Mary Magdalene who utters these three sayings of wisdom.

15. Or "She spoke this utterance as a woman who understood completely."

16. The divine world above is fullness (pleroma); this world below is deficiency.

17. Cf. Gospel of Thomas 17; 1 Cor. 2:9.

18. Cf. Gospel of the Egyptians; Dialogue of the Savior 144–45.

19. This place is the present world of deficiency and mortality.

20. Going to one's rest at once means dying now, so this may be a question about why we do not experience the transformation from death to life now, or even why we do not commit suicide now.

21. Leaving the burden of the body behind and ascending to the fullness of the divine means attaining final rest.

22. Cf. James 5:3.

23. Cf. John 14:5.

24. The archons and other powers of the cosmos.

25. On putting on the garment of the body and taking it off, cf. Dialogue of the Savior 136–39; Gospel of Mary 15; Gospel of Thomas 21; 37.

26. Possibly restore to read "[Judas]" (Petersen and Bethge, "Der Dialog des Erlösers," 395).

27. The restoration is tentative.

28. Cf. the parable of the mustard seed in Gospel of Thomas 20; Matt. 13:31–32 (Q_); Luke 13:18–19 (Q_); Mark 4:30–32.

29. Or "speaks and acts." Here the father is God the father, and the mother may be Sophia (wisdom) or another female manifestation of the divine.

30. Or "womanhood," here and below.

31. This statement seems to deny the possibility of being born again.

32. Cf. Dialogue of the Savior 140; Gospel of the Egyptians; Gospel of Thomas 114.

33. Coptic, šaje; cf. Logos.

34. Cf. Dialogue of the Savior 135.

35. Cf. Dialogue of the Savior 139.

CHAPTER SIX

1. This translation of portions of Pistis Sophia is based on the Coptic text in Pistis Sophia, ed. Carl Schmidt and Violet MacDermot (Leiden: E. J. Brill, 1978).

2. Apparently Mary Magdalene, as elsewhere in the text.

3. On the exalted place of Mary, cf. Gospel of Mary 10; 18; Gospel of Philip 59; 63–64; Pistis Sophia 19.

4. These are the archons of all the aeons—i.e., the cosmic powers who rule this world and the power of fate in this world. Here the text addresses the powers of magic and astrology, and it promises that the astrological powers will be controlled and limited in their influence.

5. Lit., in Coptic, "moaners and groaners" are "those who call from the earth and those who call from their bellies [or 'from within themselves']."

6. Cf. Isa. 19:3, 12.

7. Cf. Isa. 19:12.

8. Cf. Isa. 19:12.

9. In some gnostic texts Sabaoth (from the Lord [YHWH] Sabaoth, the Lord of Hosts) is a prominent power and a force for good. In the text

On the Origin of the World, Sabaoth is the son of the demiurge Yald-abaoth, and he despises his father and worships Pistis Sophia. Pistis Sophia in turn bestows light on him and gives him a place of great authority. Here his place on the right is such a place of honor. Cf. also the account in a Nag Hammadi text related to the text On the Origin of the World, the Reality of the Rulers (or, the Hypostasis of the Archons).

10.   On the exalted place of Mary, cf. Gospel of Mary 10; 18; Gospel of Philip 59; 63–64; Pistis Sophia 17.

11.   On the hostility of Peter toward Mary Magdalene, cf. Gospel of Mary 17–18; Gospel of Thomas 114; Pistis Sophia 72; 146. In Pistis Sophia 146 Peter says, "My master, make the women stop asking questions, so that we also may raise some questions," and Jesus responds to Mary and the women, "Give the men, your brothers, a chance to ask some questions."

12.   Pistis Sophia, a form of Sophia, repents of her mistake, which brought about a loss of light in the world of divine fullness above and brought into being her son the demiurge and this world of matter and mortality below. Eventually she is saved and restored, and with her the light and the enlightened people in this world are restored to the fullness of divinity. Pistis Sophia 87 proclaims that finally the whole human race will be brought into the kingdom of light.

13.   In Coptic, <p>ar'm'nouoein—lit., "my person of light."

14.   Cf. Gospel of Thomas 4; Matt. 20:16 (Q); Luke 13:30 (Q); Matt. 19:30; Mark 10:31; Barnabas 6:13.

15.   In Coptic, tepneumatikē 'nhilikrines—lit., "pure spiritual one" (fem.).

CHAPTER SEVEN

1.   This translation of a song from the Psalms of Heracleides is based on the Coptic text in A Manichaean Psalm-Book: Part II (Stuttgart: Kohlhammer, 1938), ed. C. R. C. Allberry, 187.

2.   Cf. John 20:1–18.

3.   Or "smallness."

4.   Cf. Gospel of Thomas 92.

CHAPTER EIGHT

(Note: For the translations of the ancient texts in this chapter, see the Revised Standard Version for biblical texts, The Nag Hammadi Library in English for the Nag Hammadi texts, and the Loeb Classical Library for Philo.)

1. Karen L. King, ed., *Images of the Feminine in Gnosticism.*

2. Anne McGuire, "Women, Gender and Gnosis in Gnostic Texts and Traditions," 288.

3. Silke Petersen, *"Zerstört die Werke der Weiblichkeit!"* 304–07.

4. For this western church portrait of Mary Magdalene, see Susan Haskins, *Mary Magdalene: Myth and Metaphor,* and Jane Schaberg, *The Resurrection of Mary Magdalene,* 65–120. The eastern church tradition celebrated her as witness to the resurrection; see Eva M. Synek, "Die andere Maria: Zum Bild der Maria von Magdala in den östlichen Kirchentraditionen." For the portrait of Mary as apostle in the western tradition at least from the eleventh century to the sixteenth century, see Katherine L. Jansen, "Maria Magdalena: Apostolorum Apostola," 57–96, and *The Making of the Magdalene.* For a short overall view, see Esther A. de Boer, *Mary Magdalene: Beyond the Myth,* 1–16.

5. There is also a Gospel of Eve.

6. Translation: R. Gryson, *Le ministère des femmes dans l'Église ancienne.* Recherches et synthèses, section d'histoire. (Gembloux: Éditions J. Duculot, S.A., 1972), 56–57. See, for the Greek text, C. Jenkins, "Origen on 1 Corinthians IV," 42. Cf. Riemer Roukema, *De uitleg van Paulus' eerste brief aan de Corinthiërs in de tweede en derde eeuw,* 218.

7. Elaine Pagels, *The Gnostic Gospels,* 77; Pheme Perkins, *The Gnostic Dialogue,* 133; Anne Pasquier, *L' Évangile selon Marie,* 24; Gilles Quispel, *Gnosis, de derde component van de Europese cultuurtraditie,* 81. In *The Woman Jesus Loved,* esp. 221–23, Antti Marjanen argues that there is no support for this usual interpretation except in the Gospel of Mary. In the Gospel of Philip there is no real controversy, in Pistis Sophia Peter's ideas are as gnostic as Mary's, and in the Gospel of Thomas the debate is not about gnosticism versus orthodoxy but about different models of asceticism.

8. In "The Gospel of Mary Magdalene," 621, Karen King calls this the image of Peter as a "continual failure." In the New Testament gospels Peter is very quick to react to Jesus and is often corrected (for instance, Mark 8:31–9:1; Mark 14:26–31, 66–72, and parallels; Matthew 14:22–33; John 21:15–23).

9. Esther A. de Boer, *Mary Magdalene: Beyond the Myth,* 92–117.

10. However, social reality was different. See Tal Ilan, *Jewish Women in Greco-Roman Palestine;* Sarah B. Pomeroy, *Goddesses, Whores, Wives, and Slaves.*

11. *The Woman Jesus Loved,* esp. 220–21. Marjanen refers to the Gospel of Thomas, the Dialogue of the Savior, the Wisdom of Jesus Christ, and the First Apocalypse of James.

12. Silke Petersen, *"Zerstört die Werke der Weiblichkeit!"* 298, also 307–08. Cf. Ingrid Maisch, *Maria Magdalena zwischen Verachtung und Verehrung,* 36.

13. See Marvin Meyer, "Making Mary Male," who refers to other texts and shows that to castigate femaleness and to recommend the transformation to maleness is by no means rare in the ancient world, and must be seen as the background of the Gospel of Thomas.

14. E.g., Grace M. Jantzen, *Power, Gender and Christian Mysticism*, 26–58.

15. See also Erika Mohri, *Maria Magdalene*, 377–78.

16. Not that Jerome was very modern in his attitude toward women, since he advocated severe asceticism. However, he had female pupils and some of his teachers were women. See Rosemary Radford Ruether, "Misogynism and Virginal Feminism in the Fathers of the Church," 150–83; Rosemary Radford Ruether, "Mothers of the Church: Ascetic Women in the Late Patristic Age," 69–98; Silvia Letsch-Brunner, *Marcella, Discipula et Magistra*.

17. Karen King, *What Is Gnosticism?* 19.

18. For a detailed exegeris of the Gospel of Mary, see Esther A. de Boer, *The Gospel of Mary: Beyond a Gnostic and a Biblical Mary Magdalene*.

19. Karen King, "The Gospel of Mary Magdalene," 601–34; Antti Marjanen, "The Mother of Jesus or the Magdalene?" 32; also Esther A. de Boer, *Mary Magdalene: Beyond the Myth*, 93, and *The Gospel of Mary*, 27–59. See also Esther A. de Boer, "A Gnostic Mary in the Gospel of Mary?"

20. Elizabeth Struthers Malbon, "Disciples / Crowds / Whoever: Markan Characters and Readers," *Novum Testamentum* 28 (1986): 104–30.

21. E.g., Luise Schottroff, "Maria Magdalena und die Frauen am Grabe Jesu," *Evangelische Theologie* 42 (1982): 3–25.

22. E.g., Schottroff, "Maria Magdalena," 3–25.

23. Turid K. Seim, *The Double Message: Patterns of Gender in Luke-Acts*, 24.

Bibliography

Aland, Kurt, ed. *Synopsis Quattuor Evangeliorum: Locis parallelis evangeliorum apoc-ryphorum et partum adhibitis.* 15th rev. ed. Corrected printing. With an appendix by the Berliner Arbeitskreis für koptisch-gnostische Schriften, "Das Thomas-Evangelium / The Gospel According to Thomas," 517–46. Stuttgart: Deutsche Bibelgesellschaft, 1996.

Allberry, C. R. C., ed. *A Manichaean Psalm-Book: Part II.* Manichaean Manu-scripts in the Chester Beatty Collection 2. Stuttgart: Kohlhammer, 1938.

Baigent, Michael, Richard Leigh, and Henry Lincoln. *Holy Blood, Holy Grail.* New York: Dell, 1983.

Barnstone, Willis, and Marvin Meyer. *The Gnostic Bible.* Boston: Shambhala, 2003.

BeDuhn, Jason. *The Manichaean Body: In Discipline and Ritual.* Baltimore: Johns Hopkins Univ. Press, 2000.

Blatz, Beate, and Einar Thomassen. "The Dialogue of the Savior." In *New Tes-tament Apocrypha,* edited by Wilhelm Schneemelcher, 1:300–312. Cam-bridge: James Clarke; Louisville: Westminster/John Knox, 1991–92.

Bovon, François. "Mary Magdalene in the *Acts of Philip.*" In *Which Mary?,* edited by F. Stanley Jones, 75–89. Atlanta: Society of Biblical Litera-ture, 2002.

Bovon, François, Bertrand Bouvier, and Frédéric Amsler, eds. *Acta Philippi: Textus.* Corpus Christianorum series apocryphorum 11. Turnhout: Bre-pols, 1999.

Brock, Ann Graham. *Mary Magdalene, the First Apostle: The Struggle for Authority.* Harvard Theological Studies 51. Cambridge: Harvard Univ. Press, 2002.

Brooten, Bernadette. *Women Leaders in the Ancient Synagogue: Inscriptional Evidence and Background Issues.* Brown Judaic Studies 36. Chico, CA: Scholars Press, 1982.

Brown, Dan. *The Da Vinci Code: A Novel.* New York: Doubleday, 2003.

Brown, Raymond E. *The Gospel According to John.* Anchor Bible 29–29A. Garden City, NY: Doubleday, 1966–70.

Bultmann, Rudolph. *The Gospel of John: A Commentary.* Translated by G. R. Beasley-Murray, R. W. N. Hoare, and J. K. Riches. Philadelphia: Westminster, 1971.

Crossan, John Dominic. *The Cross That Spoke: The Origins of the Passion Narrative.* San Francisco: Harper & Row, 1988.

———. *Four Other Gospels: Shadows on the Contours on Canon.* Minneapolis: Winston (Seabury), 1985.

de Boer, Esther A. *The Gospel of Mary: Beyond a Gnostic and a Biblical Mary Magdalene.* Journal for the Study of the New Testament, Supplemental Series 260. London: T. & T. Clark (Continuum), 2004.

———. "A Gnostic Mary in the Gospel of Mary?" In *Proceedings of the Seventh International Congress of Coptic Studies,* Orientalia Lovaniensia Analecta, edited by J. van der Vliet. Louvain: Peeters, 2004.

———. "Mary Magdalene and the Disciple Jesus Loved." *Lectio Difficilior* 1 (2000). http://www.lectio.unibe.ch.

———. *Mary Magdalene: Beyond the Myth.* Translated by John Bowden. Harrisburg, PA: Trinity Press International, 1997.

DeConick, April D. "The Great Mystery of Marriage: Sex and Conception in Ancient Valentinian Traditions." *Vigiliae Christianae* 57 (2003): 307–42.

Eisen, Ute E. *Amtsträgerinnen im frühen Christentum: Epigraphische und literarische Studien.* Forschungen zur Kirchen- und Dogmengeschichte 61. Göttingen: Vandenhoeck & Ruprecht, 1996.

Emmel, Stephen, ed. *Nag Hammadi Codex III,5: The Dialogue of the Savior.* Nag Hammadi Studies 26. Leiden: E. J. Brill, 1984.

Fredriksson, Marianne. *According to Mary Magdalene.* Translated by Joanne Tate. Charlottesville, NC: Hampton Roads, 1999.

Fuchs, Albert. *Das Petrusevangelium: Mit 2 Beiträgen von F. Weißengruber und unter Mitarbeitung von Chr. Eckmair.* Studien zum Neuen Testament und seiner Umwelt, B 2. Linz: F. Plochl, 1978.

Good, Deirdre. "Pistis Sophia." In *Searching the Scriptures: A Feminist Commentary,* edited by Elisabeth Schüssler Fiorenza, 2:678–707. New York: Crossroad, 1993–94.

Gryson, Roger. *Le ministère des femmes dans l'Église ancienne.* Recherches et synthèses, Section d'histoire. Gembloux: Éditions J. Duculot, S.A., 1972.

Haskins, Susan. *Mary Magdalene: Myth and Metaphor.* New York: Harcourt Brace & Co., 1993.

Ilan, Tal. *Jewish Women in Greco-Roman Palestine: An Inquiry into Image and Status.* Texte und Studien zum Antiken Judentum 44. Tübingen: J. C. B. Mohr (Paul Siebeck), 1995.

Jansen, Katherine L. *The Making of the Magdalene: Preaching and Popular Devotion in the Later Middle Ages.* Princeton: Princeton Univ. Press, 2000.

———. "Maria Magdalena: Apostolorum Apostola." In *Women Preachers and Prophets Through Two Millennia of Christianity,* edited by Beverly M. Kienzle and Pamela J. Walker, 57–96. Berkeley: Univ. of California Press, 1998.

Jantzen, Grace M. *Power, Gender, and Christian Mysticism.* Cambridge Studies in Ideology and Religion 8. Cambridge and New York: Cambridge Univ. Press, 1997.

Jenkins, C. "Origen on 1 Corinthians IV." *Journal of Theological Studies* 10 (1909): 29–51.

Jensen, Anne. *Gottes selbstbewusste Töchter: Frauenemanzipation im frühen Christentum?* Freiburg, Basel, and Vienna: Herder, 1992.

Jones, F. Stanley, ed. *Which Mary? The Marys of Early Christian Tradition.* Symposium 19. Atlanta: Society of Biblical Literature, 2002.

Kazantzakis, Nikos. *The Last Temptation of Christ.* Translated by P. A. Bien. New York: Simon & Schuster, 1960.

King, Karen L. "The Gospel of Mary." In *The Complete Gospels,* edited by Robert J. Miller, 361–66. Santa Rosa, CA: Polebridge, 1994.

———. "The Gospel of Mary Magdalene." In *Searching the Scriptures: A Feminist Commentary,* edited by Elisabeth Schüssler Fiorenza, 601–34. London: SCM Press, 1995.

———. *The Gospel of Mary of Magdala: Jesus and the First Woman Apostle.* Santa Rosa, CA: Polebridge, 2003.

———. *What Is Gnosticism?* Cambridge: Harvard Univ. Press/Belknap, 2003.

———. "Why All the Controversy? Mary in the *Gospel of Mary.*" In *Which Mary?,* edited by F. Stanley Jones, 53–74. Atlanta: Society of Biblical Literature, 2002.

———, ed. *Images of the Feminine in Gnosticism.* Studies in Antiquity and Christianity. Philadelphia: Fortress, 1988.

Klimkeit, Hans-Joachim. *Gnosis on the Silk Road: Gnostic Texts from Central Asia.* San Francisco: HarperSanFrancisco, 1993.

Koester, Helmut. *Ancient Christian Gospels: Their History and Development.* Philadelphia: Trinity; London: SCM Press, 1990.

Koester, Helmut, and Elaine H. Pagels. Introduction to *Nag Hammadi Codex III,5: The Dialogue of the Savior,* edited by Stephen Emmel. Leiden: E. J. Brill, 1984.

Layton, Bentley. *The Gnostic Scriptures.* Garden City, NY: Doubleday, 1987.
———, ed. *Nag Hammadi Codex II,2–7, Together with XIII,2*, Brit. Lib. Or. 4926(1), and P. Oxy. 1, 654, 655.* 2 vols. Nag Hammadi Studies 20–21. Leiden: E. J. Brill, 1989.

Letsch-Brunner, Silvia. *Marcella, Discipula et Magistra: Auf den Spuren einer römischen Christin des 4. Jahrhunderts.* Beihefte zur Zeitschrift für die neutestamentliche Wissenschaft und die Kunde der älteren Kirche 91. Berlin and New York: Walter de Gruyter, 1998.

Mack, Burton. *A Myth of Innocence: Mark and Christian Origins.* Philadelphia: Fortress, 1988.

Maisch, Ingrid. *Maria Magdalena zwischen Verachtung und Verehrung: Das Bild einer Frau im Spiegel der Jahrhunderte.* Freiburg, Basel, and Vienna: Herder, 1996.

Mara, Maria Grazia. *Évangile de Pierre: Introduction, texte critique, traduction, commentaire, et index.* Sources chrétiennes 201. Paris: Cerf, 1973.

Marjanen, Antti. "The Mother of Jesus or the Magdalene? The Identity of Mary in the So-Called Gnostic Christian Texts." In *Which Mary?*, edited by F. Stanley Jones, 31–42. Atlanta: Society of Biblical Literature, 2002.

———. *The Woman Jesus Loved: Mary Magdalene in the Nag Hammadi Library and Related Documents.* Nag Hammadi and Manichaean Studies 40. Leiden: E. J. Brill, 1996.

McGuire, Anne. "Virginity and Subversion: Norea Against the Powers in *Hypostasis of the Archons.*" In *Images of the Feminine in Gnosticism,* edited by Karen L. King, 239–58. Philadelphia: Fortress, 1988.

———. "Women, Gender, and Gnosis in Gnostic Texts and Traditions." In *Women and Christian Origins,* edited by Ross S. Kraemer and Mary Rose D'Angelo, 257–99. Oxford and New York: Oxford Univ. Press, 1999.

Ménard, Jacques É. *L'Évangile selon Philippe: Introduction, texte, traduction, commentaire.* Strasbourg and Paris: Letouzey & Ané, 1967.

Meyer, Marvin. *The Gospel of Thomas: The Hidden Sayings of Jesus.* San Francisco: HarperCollins, 1992.

———. "*Gospel of Thomas* Logion 114 Revisited." In *For the Children, Perfect Instruction: Studies in Honor of Hans-Martin Schenke on the Occasion of the Berliner Arbeitskreis für koptisch-gnostische Schriften's Thirtieth Year,* edited by Hans-Gebhard Bethge, Stephen Emmel, Karen L. King, and Imke Schletterer, 101–11. Nag Hammadi and Manichaean Studies 54. Leiden: E.J. Brill, 2002. Also in *Secret Gospels,* by Marvin Meyer, 96–106. Harrisburg, PA; London; and New York: Trinity Press International/Continuum, 2003.

———. "Making Mary Male: The Categories 'Male' and 'Female' in the *Gospel of Thomas.*" *New Testament Studies* 31 (1985): 544–70. Pp. 76–95 in Marvin Meyer, *Secret Gospels.*

———. *Secret Gospels: Essays on Thomas and the Secret Gospel of Mark.* Harrisburg, PA; London; and New York: Trinity Press International/Continuum, 2003.

Meyers, Carol, Toni Craven, and Ross S. Kraemer, eds. *Women in Scripture: A Dictionary of Named and Unnamed Women in the Hebrew Bible, the Apocryphal/ Deuterocanonical Books, and the New Testament.* Grand Rapids, MI, and Cambridge, U.K.: Eerdmans, 2001.

Miller, Robert J., ed. *The Complete Gospels: Annotated Scholars Version.* Santa Rosa, CA: Polebridge, 1994.

Mohri, Erika. *Maria Magdalena: Frauenbilder in Evangelientexten des 1. bis 3. Jahrhunderts.* Marburger Theologischen Studien 63. Marburg: N.G. Elwert Verlag, 2000.

Osiek, Carolyn. "Mary 3" [Mary Magdalene]. In *Women in Scripture,* edited by Carol Meyers, Toni Craven, and Ross S. Kraemer, 120–23. Grand Rapids, MI, and Cambridge, U.K.: Eerdmans, 2001.

Pagels, Elaine H. *Beyond Belief: The Secret Gospel of Thomas.* New York: Random House, 2003.

———. *The Gnostic Gospels.* New York: Random House, 1981.

Pasquier, Anne. *L'Évangile selon Marie (BG 1).* Bibliothèque copte de Nag Hammadi, Section "Textes" 10. Quebec: Les presses de l'Université Laval, 1983.

Patterson, Stephen J. *The Gospel of Thomas and Jesus.* Foundations and Facets. Santa Rosa, CA: Polebridge, 1993.

Patterson, Stephen J., James M. Robinson, and Hans-Gebhard Bethge. *The Fifth Gospel: The Gospel of Thomas Comes of Age.* Harrisburg, PA: Trinity Press International, 1998.

Pearson, Birger. "Revisiting Norea." In *Images of the Feminine in Gnosticism,* edited by Karen L. King, 265–75. Philadelphia: Fortress, 1988.

Perkins, Pheme. *The Gnostic Dialogue: The Early Church and the Crisis of Gnosticism.* New York: Paulist Press, 1980.

———. "Sophia as Goddess in the Nag Hammadi Codices." In *Images of the Feminine in Gnosticism,* edited by Karen L. King, 96–112. Philadelphia: Fortress, 1988.

Petersen, Silke. *"Zerstört die Werke der Weiblichkeit!" Maria Magdalena, Salome und andere Jüngerinnen Jesu in christlich-gnostischen Schriften.* Nag Hammadi and Manichaean Studies 48. Leiden: E. J. Brill, 1999.

Petersen, Silke, and Hans-Gebhard Bethge. "Der Dialog des Erlösers." In *Nag Hammadi Deutsch. 1. Band,* edited by Hans-Martin Schenke, Hans-Gebhard Bethge, and Ursula Ulrike Kaiser, 381–97. Berlin and New York: Walter de Gruyter, 2001.